Teaching
INCLUSIVE
Mathematics
to Special Learners, K-6

In loving memory of Sten

JULIE A. SLIVA

Teaching
INCLUSIVE
Mathematics
to Special Learners, K-6

CORWIN PRESS, INC.
A Sage Publications Company
Thousand Oaks, California

For information:

Corwin Press, Inc.
A Sage Publications Company
2455 Teller Road
Thousand Oaks, California 91320
www.corwinpress.com

Sage Publications Ltd.
6 Bonhill Street
London EC2A 4PU
United Kingdom

Sage Publications India Pvt. Ltd.
B-42, Panchsheel Enclave
Post Box 4109
New Delhi 110 017 India

Printed in the United States of America

Library of Congress Cataloging-in-Publication Data

Sliva, Julie A.
Teaching inclusive mathematics to special learners, K-6 / Julie Sliva.
    p. cm.
Includes bibliographical references and index.
ISBN 0-7619-3890-7 (acid-free paper) — ISBN 0-7619-3891-5 (pbk. :: acid-free paper)
    1. Mathematics—Study and teaching (Elementary)
2. Learning disabled children—Education (Elementary) I. Title.
QA135.6.S57 2004
371.9´0447—dc22

                                    2003014412

This book is printed on acid-free paper.

03   04   05   06   07   10   9   8   7   6   5   4   3   2   1

Acquisitions editor:	Jean Ward
Production editor:	Sanford Robinson
Copy editor:	Teresa Herlinger
Typesetter:	C&M Digitals (P) Ltd.
Proofreader:	Tricia Toney
Cover designer:	Tracy Miller
Graphic designer:	Lisa Miller
Indexer:	Monica Smersh

Contents

About the Author

 **Julie A. Sliva** brings to this topic a rich background in mathematics, technology, and special education. As an assistant professor of mathematics education at San Jose State University, she teaches methods of mathematics instruction to aspiring educators and supervises their field experiences. Julie continues to enjoy inservice work with teachers grades K–12. Julie's research interests include studying teacher and student attitudes toward teaching and learning mathematics, and best practices for teaching mathematics to special needs learners. She is a frequent presenter at the National Council of Teachers of Mathematics Annual Meetings, the California Mathematics Annual Conference, and the International Group for the Psychology of Mathematics Education, North American Chapter.

Acknowledgments

Corwin Press gratefully acknowledges the contributions of the following reviewers:

Melissa Adams
Director of Primary Mathematics
Silicon Valley Mathematics Initiative
Gilroy, California

Karen Currier
Principal, Ranch View School
Naperville, Illinois

Dr. Timothy J. McNamara
Assistant Professor of Mathematics
Monroe Community College
Rochester, New York

Dr. Cecil Mercer
Distinguished Professor
University of Florida
Gainesville, Florida

Meg Ormiston
President, TechTeachers
Hinsdale, Illinois

Larry Osthus
Mathematics Consultant
Heartland Area Education Agency 11
Johnston, Iowa

Introduction

The education of all children, regardless of background or disability . . . must always be a national priority. One of the most important goals of my administration is to support states and local communities in creating and maintaining a system of public education where no child is left behind. Unfortunately, among those at greatest risk of being left behind are children with disabilities.

President George W. Bush,
Executive Order 13227

The demands on the K–6 teacher have changed dramatically over the past decade. These teachers are faced with an increasingly wide range of academic abilities in their classrooms. while having to stay abreast of district, state, and National Standards for teaching mathematics and other subject areas. New technologies require teachers to be familiar with latest technology and to know how to meaningfully integrate these new technologies into their curricula. In addition, an increase in the numbers of special education students in the general education classroom presents a further daily challenge. Put simply, teachers are charged with the task of "leaving no child behind" at a time when the challenges are greater than ever, and more and more students are vulnerable to being left.

This book is written for teachers of students with difficulties learning mathematics. These may be special education teachers, elementary teachers who teach all content areas including mathematics, teachers having special responsibility for teaching mathematics on an elementary team, or school mathematics specialists who want to provide help for their teachers teaching mathematics. The purpose of this book is to provide an expanded framework of understanding for K–6 educators to use when teaching their students who are having difficulties learning mathematics. This book will describe recent research on students with learning disabilities and the impact these difficulties may have on their learning of mathematics, and it will offer strategies for instruction to facilitate their learning. This book will specifically discuss strategies for teaching students with disabilities. However, many of these strategies are useful for teaching all students, including low-achieving students in the regular education classroom.

This book will describe in detail the characteristics of students with learning disabilities as a means to help teachers "see inside the heads," of their most challenged students and better understand the difficulties they experience. The book will provide a process of gathering information about students with learning difficulties. It will offer strategies to compensate for specific learning difficulties, as well as general strategies for instruction that benefit all students, in particular those students with difficulties learning mathematics.

While reading this book, those educators who are already teaching students whose difficulties puzzle them will probably find themselves thinking about these students and how the ideas presented here might apply to helping these children. To this end, this book will introduce three students, Amanda, Dominick, and Elizabeth, in Chapter 1.

Amanda has always felt like a failure in mathematics and that she was just "not good" at mathematics. Amanda has attention problems; she is diagnosed with attention deficit/hyperactivity disorder (AD/HD) and has taken the drug Ritalin for the past four years.

Dominick says he likes math, and from class work his teacher believes that he understands quite a bit. This is confusing to his teacher because he has a lot of trouble taking tests and quizzes, failing most of them weekly.

Elizabeth is a very quiet fourth-grade student. She has developed fluency with her math facts; however, she consistently has difficulties when solving word problems.

The reader will see these students reappear as example students for applying ideas in this book. The assessment chapter will provide a completed observation for each of these students so that you may see an example of how one process for assessing your students with learning difficulties can be accomplished. Other students will appear briefly throughout the book.

The book is organized to take the reader from an overview and an acquaintance with the Individualized Education Plan (IEP) process, to deeper understanding of specific difficulties and strategies, to a tool for more productive observation of students and what they may need, to the ultimate goal of providing standards-based mathematics learning for all students. For teachers who don't yet have such students in their classrooms, envisioning how the ideas would apply to particular students while reading this book might be helpful. This will give readers an "organizer" with which to clarify understanding, observation, and strategy selection for their students. A description of the chapter content follows.

CHAPTER ONE: TEACHING THE CHALLENGED LEARNER

This chapter introduces Amanda, Dominick, and Elizabeth, students who have difficulties learning mathematics. It discusses recent research on students with learning difficulties in mathematics, as well as special-education legislation and its importance for the teacher. The chapter will also detail the process by which a student is determined eligible for special-education services and provide guidance to assist the teacher when gathering information to plan for instruction. Finally, it will present information about the possible role(s) a paraprofessional may play in the mathematics classroom.

CHAPTER TWO: CHARACTERISTICS OF STUDENTS WITH LEARNING DISABILITIES AND THE IMPACT ON LEARNING MATHEMATICS

This chapter discusses research about typical characteristics of students with learning disabilities and how these may impact their learning of mathematics. Specifically, the chapter describes learning difficulties in the areas of

- Information processing
  - Visual deficits
  - Auditory-processing difficulties
  - Motor disabilities
  - Memory deficits
  - Attention deficits
- Language
  - Expressive
  - Receptive
- Cognitive and metacognitive issues
- Maintaining positive attitudes toward learning mathematics

CHAPTER THREE: SPECIFIC STRATEGIES FOR INSTRUCTION

This chapter examines each of the areas that can impact a student's learning of mathematics, and suggests multiple compensatory strategies to address each of these areas of difficulty. It also offers tips for helping students understand textbooks and complete their homework successfully. A reproducible matrix of difficulties and strategies is provided, which teachers may use to keep track of what works best in teaching particular students.

CHAPTER FOUR: ASSESSING YOUR SPECIAL EDUCATION STUDENT

This chapter discusses a framework for assessing your students who have difficulties learning mathematics. A reproducible observation checklist of "look fors" is included. Completed examples are shown for Amanda, Dominick, and Elizabeth. This assessment offers a baseline from which to build improved learning for any student. For students with complex learning disabilities, it will provide the basis for productive conversation with building specialists about how to better include these students.

CHAPTER FIVE: GENERAL STRATEGIES FOR TEACHING INCLUSIVE MATHEMATICS TO ALL STUDENTS

The final chapter for this book discusses strategies for teaching mathematics as suggested by the National Council of Teachers of Mathematics (NCTM) and research that supports the learning of mathematics for all students. Students with a wide range of difficulties learning mathematics, including learning disabilities, will benefit from the strategies presented throughout this chapter.

Teaching students who have difficulties learning mathematics can seem at first to be a very challenging task. However, as a teacher becomes aware of the specific areas of difficulty for students, develops a repertoire of possible compensatory strategies, coupled with research-based strategies for teaching students mathematics, the task of teaching these students can be successfully accomplished. The challenge is significant, but the rewards are in the increased teaching satisfaction and the joy of watching students grow in competency and self-understanding.

Teaching the 1 Challenged Learner

It is the first day of school and you have been told that your new class will contain twenty-eight students, five who qualify for special education services. How do you begin to plan for instruction to meet the needs of your special education students? What are the difficulties that these students may encounter while learning mathematics? And, what are the strategies that can be used to best facilitate their understandings of mathematics?

Amanda, Dominick, and Elizabeth may have some characteristics of students that you have previously taught. They are composites of students and are not meant to encompass all of the learning disabilities that will be discussed in this and coming chapters. Rather, these students represent a few of the possible combinations of learning disabilities that a teacher may encounter at any grade level. This chapter will introduce these three students and describe the impact their disabilities have on their mathematical understanding. It will describe recent research findings regarding students with learning disabilities and their learning of mathematics. In addition to introducing these students whom you may recognize from your own school, this chapter will also describe the teacher's responsibility regarding the process of teaching students with disabilities and the requirements placed on teachers by legislation. As you read this text and the suggestions for learning-disabled students, low achievers, and discouraged students, it may be helpful to have these concrete examples of students in mind. If you have inclusive students of your own, as you read this text, keep those students in mind and how these suggestions may apply to them.

MEET AMANDA

Amanda is a personable, mature sixth-grade student who works very hard on homework for each of her classes. She is often assisted in this daily endeavor by a patient and supportive mother. Amanda felt success in mathematics only once in elementary school. She attributed all of her success that year to her third-grade teacher. Except for her experience in third grade, Amanda has always considered herself a failure in mathematics. Amanda defines herself as someone who is "not good"at math. She has been diagnosed with attention deficit disorder (AD/HD) and has taken the drug Ritalin for the past four years. She knows that she has problems focusing and paying attention in class but does not know how to help herself. As a result, Amanda seems to get very little from her daily classroom mathematics instruction. To help alleviate this problem, Amanda works with a math tutor and with her parents to gain more understanding of mathematics. However, this has not significantly helped her grades, as she still is failing most of her chapter exams. At times, she will do remarkably well on quizzes; she attributes this to "luck."

Amanda has difficulty completing mathematics tests in the required amount of time. In addition, she often will confuse information on a test, combining pieces from one problem with information from another problem. Frequently, Amanda forgets to do her homework or to bring it to school (especially if her mother is busy herself the night before). She misplaces important papers, assignment sheets, and other needed materials.

Amanda enjoys working on problems that can be solved in a sequential manner and is very adept at using her calculator to check her work. Spatially, Amanda's skills appear to be age appropriate. She enjoys working with other students and is always willing to contribute to the small-group discussion. However, she is usually very quiet outside a small-group setting. What can Amanda's teacher do to help her gain confidence in her math skills class and become a more successful student?

MEET DOMINICK

Dominick is an energetic seven-and-a-half-year-old second-grade student. He was adopted from an orphanage in Asia when he was three and is currently experiencing some language problems. Dominick has trouble expressing himself in class. He becomes visibly distressed when asked to explain his answers. Dominick's verbal responses are unorganized, use endings incorrectly, and lack appropriate syntax. Dominick also has some attention problems. He often does not appear to listen in class; perhaps because he does not fully understand all that is asked of him.

Dominick works well in a cooperative learning environment. He makes friends easily. However, when working independently, he frequently has a hard time getting started on assignments without assistance. His mathematics skills are below average. His computation is on grade level. He can add and subtract well, as long as he correctly interprets the signs. His spatial skills are strong. However, his word-problem-solving skills are much weaker. This is no doubt due, in part, to his delayed progress in reading. He seems to understand concepts such as time, basic measurement, and money, but has difficulty with place value, understanding the concept of equality, and problems involving words. His work on standardized tests is poor. Dominick says he likes mathematics, and from his class work, his teacher believes that he understands more than he is able to apply. Dominick has a lot of trouble taking tests and quizzes; failing most of them weekly. Other students easily distract him. He lacks the patience or perseverance to finish up assignments. He has difficulty completing daily homework. His locker lacks organization. He cannot locate needed books, papers, or materials when necessary.

Dominick enjoys sports and has been taking tennis lessons for a few years. He plays very well for his age.

How can Dominick's teacher best help him understand mathematics?

MEET ELIZABETH

Elizabeth is a very quiet fourth-grade student. She comes into class quietly and complies with requests without fussing or arguing. She turns in homework most days, but many problems are incorrect or incomplete. Although class time is given to reviewing these problems, Elizabeth never asks a question. In fact, she avoids eye contact with her teacher, and relates comfortably with only two other girls in the class. She is often absent on test or quiz days and makes no effort to make up these graded assessments.

Elizabeth can recite her mathematics facts and uses them for math computation efficiently. Her weaknesses are primarily in the area of solving word problems. When she begins the process of problem solving, she tends to have difficulty analyzing the question and developing a plan to solve the problem. At times, she cannot seem to remember having seen a similar type of problem. She has relatively good success with solving a word problem once she has guided support with setting the problem up. Spatially, Elizabeth seems to have strong skills, even in relation to other students in the class.

Often, Elizabeth seems to be daydreaming. Her teacher has stated that she appears to be a very self-conscious student. Elizabeth is nervous, she cannot relax in class, and frequently bites her nails. Elizabeth loves cats. Her parents say she spends a great deal of time reading information in books and online about how to care for her cat. In addition, she loves to draw; usually she draws animals.

What teaching strategies would best serve Elizabeth's mathematics needs?

CURRENT TRENDS IN SPECIAL EDUCATION

In the past, there were few special education students in regular education mathematics classes; many were pulled out for instruction or extra support and placed in resource rooms. However, this has dramatically changed. Increasingly, there are larger numbers of special education students like Amanda, Dominick, and Elizabeth in the regular education mathematics classes. It is the inclusion of these students in the legally required "least restrictive environment," which in most cases is the regular classroom, that has prompted use of the terms "inclusion" and "inclusive classroom." This movement toward increased inclusion, due in part to legislative mandates and trends in special education, has seen regular education classrooms accommodate greater numbers of students with disabilities, while fewer students with more severe needs are educated in separate school settings (McLeskey, Henry, & Hodges, 1999). At the same time, as more students with disabilities are being included in the regular education classroom, mathematics requirements are being increased. The National Council of Teachers of Mathematics (NCTM) in the 2000 *Principles and Standards for School Mathematics*, relates a vision for the future of mathematics

> In which all students have access to rigorous, high-quality mathematics instruction, including four years of high school mathematics, [and in which] the curriculum is mathematically rich, providing students with opportunities to learn important mathematical concepts and procedures with understanding. (NCTM, 2000b, p. 1)

This reform movement advocates constructivism for teaching mathematics. In the mathematics classroom, students are to be complementing their basic computational skill knowledge with more of an emphasis on solving challenging, open-ended word problems that can be solved using a variety of methods. To do well in reform-based mathematics, students are required to reason mathematically, and to explain their thinking to others in an attempt to construct personally meaningful understandings of mathematical concepts.

Several states have legislated that all students must pass algebra I to graduate from high school. New trends in middle-grades mathematics are also contributing to changes in what is taught in the classroom. In many schools, a shift has begun from teaching algebra in the ninth grade to teaching algebra in the eighth grade, and pre-algebra in the seventh grade. As a result, it has become even more important that K–8 students learn mathematics in a meaningful manner so that their conceptual understandings prepare them for learning higher level mathematics. In addition, because mathematics has become a gatekeeper to a number of opportunities for occupational and educational advancement (Jetter, 1993), it is more important than ever that all of our students obtain understandings of higher level mathematics.

Students with learning disabilities (LD) frequently have difficulty with mathematics computation and problem solving. Numerous investigators have found that students with learning disabilities experience even greater difficulty in math than their peers without disabilities (Ackerman, Anhalt, & Dykman, 1986; McLeod & Armstrong, 1982). Cawley, Parmar, Yan, and Miller (1998) found that while normally achieving students learn mathematics concepts in a steadily increasing pattern, students with learning disabilities acquire skills in a broken sequence and have lower retention rates than their non-disabled peers, and these lower retention rates increase as the concepts become more difficult. In addition, these researchers (1998) found that students ages 9 to 14 with learning disabilities demonstrated very little progress in computation from one year to the next. Students with and without learning disabilities who have problems learning mathematics usually begin experiencing these difficulties in elementary school, and then continue through secondary school into adulthood. The statistics regarding math performance among students with learning disabilities are alarming. Cawley and Miller (1989) reported that 8- and 9-year-olds with learning disabilities performed at about a first-grade level on computation and application.

It is essential that elementary students be helped to develop solid mathematical understanding in early grades in order to provide the groundwork for success rather than failure. In many schools, however, it is especially difficult for students with disabilities to obtain the necessary level of math proficiency due to issues related to tracking. Historically, special education students encounter difficulties early on in their mathematical career, and then are not able to reach a higher level of mathematics because of placement in courses focusing on basic skills rather than upper-level math. It has become more important than ever that these students gain a solid background in elementary mathematics.

Mathematics deficiencies of students with learning problems emerge in the early years and continue throughout secondary school. Studies have shown that the mathematical knowledge of students with learning problems progresses about one year for each two years of school attendance (Cawley & Miller, 1989), and their mathematics progress reaches a plateau after seventh grade (Warner, Alley, Schumaker, Deshler, & Clark, 1980). These studies report that the mean scores of special education students in the twelfth grade were at the high fifth-grade level.

Traditional mathematics curricula, especially those designed for special education students, emphasize computational routines and memorization of basic facts (Mastropieri, Scruggs, & Shiah, 1991; Parmar, Cawley, & Frazita, 1996; Thornton & Jones, 1996). Special education students typically experience early failure in mathematics, after which they are often placed in classes focusing on a more traditional, less challenging curriculum of basic mathematics skills versus classes that contain higher level mathematics and emphasize conceptual learning (Shriner, Kim, Thurlow, & Ysseldyke, 1993; Thornton & Jones, 1996). In particular, students with disabilities are not involved with on-going problem-solving experiences in mathematics, which also limits the opportunities for them to engage in discussions about their own mathematical thinking (Haberman, 1991). As a result, many of these students never experience a conceptually higher level of mathematics and are left out of reform-based mathematics (Baxter, Woodward, & Olson, 2001).

As a counterpoint to this sad record, encouraging research has found that students with mathematical disabilities can improve their mathematical performance (Mastropieri, Scruggs, & Shiah, 1991; Rivera & Smith, 1988). Specifically, research has indicated that students with disabilities can improve their computational and mathematics reasoning skills when they are taught using a problem-solving curriculum that engages them in learning mathematics by experiencing and thinking about meaningful problems (Speer & Brahier, 1994). Further, Marolda (2000) states that "children with learning disabilities can learn effectively and with better long-term results when conceptually oriented instruction is offered in a balanced and comprehensive fashion, using the child's strengths to shore up the weaknesses" (p. 4).

As the integration of students with disabilities into the general education classroom increases, many teachers are struggling to meet the needs of an academically heterogeneous classroom.

The task of teaching students with learning difficulties in mathematics is indeed challenging and may seem daunting; however, by becoming more aware of how specific disabilities interfere with learning and of strategies that can mitigate the difficulties, teachers can grow in confidence in approaching this complex task. Both teachers and disabled students will find greater satisfaction as teachers adopt new approaches that go beyond the worksheets and computational drills that have been the default approach with special education students and low achievers. Ultimately teachers can begin to help special education students to recognize strategies that are personally helpful and to internalize them for use in other classes and in life.

It is helpful for a teacher to become familiar with legal responsibilities and procedures regarding having a student who receives special services in their class. The following sections will describe legislation related to students with disabilities and the impact of these on the regular education teacher.

Recent Special-education Legislation

In 1975, the Education for All Handicapped Children Act (Public Law 94–142) was passed and guaranteed that all students with disabilities would receive a public education. The law, whose name changed in subsequent reauthorizations in both 1990 and 1997 to the Individuals With Disabilities Education Act (IDEA), was the beginning of a movement toward inclusive schooling, and ruled that every child is eligible to receive a free and appropriate education in the least restrictive environment. IDEA mandated that federal funding be given to state and local agencies for the purpose of providing special education and related services to qualified students. Children and adolescents between the ages of 3 and 21 who are deemed eligible by a multidisciplinary team (teacher, administrator, school psychologist, special education instructor, parent) would now be able to receive academic assistance. Students qualifying for special education services must be eligible in one or more of the following thirteen categories: autism, deaf-blindness, deafness, emotional disturbance, hearing impairment, mental retardation, multiple disabilities, orthopedic impairment, other health impairment, specific learning disability, speech or language impairment, traumatic brain injury, and visual impairment including blindness. Children 3 through 9 experiencing developmental delays may also be eligible.

Around the same time, Section 504 of the Rehabilitation Act of 1973 and the Americans With Disabilities Act (ADA) of 1990 were also passed. These legislative acts are designed to protect the civil rights of individuals with disabilities and prevent any form of discrimination against these individuals. Both of these acts are now receiving a great deal of attention from schools because many parents are beginning to request services for children who are not eligible for them under IDEA. Due to the fact that Section 504 and the ADA have different definitions of disability, many children who are not provided services under IDEA may be eligible to receive services under one of these acts (Smith, 2001). The following are examples of disabilities likely covered by Section 504 and not IDEA: students who have low IQ scores but do not qualify as having mental retardation; students with orthopedic problems who do not need special education; students with communicable diseases such as AIDS or hepatitis; and students with learning disabilities whose discrepancy between intellectual ability and achievement is not significant enough for IDEA eligibility.

Most recently, there is a trend toward "inclusion"—fully including all special education students in the general education classroom. This movement supports the philosophy that all special education students should be educated in regular education classes all of the time. Inclusion involves placement of students in their neighborhood school, with individuals their own age, in the regular education environment with appropriate support services such as aides and curricular adaptations. Inclusion assumes that these students are never segregated and their base or home in the school is the regular classroom (Schulz & Carpenter, 1995).

The Individualized Education Plan (IEP) Process

An IEP is a written commitment of individualized services, which assures that special education and related services will be received. By law, the IEP must include information about the student and the educational program designed to meet his/her needs. These plans typically include information such as tests used to identify the student as having a disability; the student's areas of weakness; the specific plan of action to be taken to achieve growth in each of the deficit areas identified; and any special services the student will receive from the school—accommodations and modifications, as well as the person who will deliver these services.

From a practical standpoint, IEPs do not always provide information that is necessary to the teacher. For example, the IEP offers limited help in understanding a student. Although the IEPs contain benchmarks and goals for what a student is to achieve, they do not often offer strategies to help students achieve these benchmarks.

Any teacher who teaches a student who receives special education services will receive a copy of the child's IEP. The development of a student's IEP is part of the larger special education process under IDEA. The following section will describe a typical process used to identify a student with a disability, commonly referred to as the pre-referral process and the writing of the IEP.

What does the regular classroom teacher need to know from the IEP?

The classroom teacher needs to know what the IEP states regarding her responsibilities for the student. The following required components of an IEP are beneficial to the regular classroom teacher when teaching a student with disabilities: The student's current levels of educational performance, measurable goals and objectives or benchmarks, special education and related services, the extent of participation with non-disabled children, a statement of how the student's progress will be measured and how the parents will be informed of that progress, the extent of modifications of participation in state and districtwide tests, and the dates and location of services to be provided.

Figure 1.1   Sample: Critical Mathematics IEP Information Sheet

---

Student Name: Jacqueline Anderson   **Age:** <u>8</u>

Current levels of educational performance in mathematics:
Jacqueline has a limited understanding of place value. She is able to correctly identify the ones and tens place. She knows her multiplication facts for 0–2s, and her doubles. Jacqueline can also identify several common shapes such as a square, triangle, and circle. She has difficulty solving word problems. Jacqueline can write numbers legibly and has no difficulty with reversals.

Measurable goals:
Jacqueline will be able to understand and apply multiplication facts to correctly solve problems through 7×9.
Jacqueline will be able to understand and apply knowledge of place value including the hundreds place, thousands place, up to one million.
Jacqueline will be able to correctly set up and solve word problems using multiplication facts and place-value skills that she has mastered.

Measurable objectives or benchmarks:
Jacqueline will write or state verbally her multiplication facts from 0 to 7×9 with 90% accuracy.
Jacqueline will correctly set up and solve word problems involving multiplication facts with 90% accuracy.
Jacqueline will be able to verbally or in written form correctly identify the value of a given numeral in a number including thousands with 90% accuracy.

Special education and related services:
Jacqueline will receive support services from a special educator in her regular mathematics classroom three times a week for 50 minutes. This class will be co-taught and planned by the regular education teacher and the special educator.

The extent of participation with non-disabled children:
Jacqueline should be placed in the regular education classroom for her mathematics instruction and have normal interaction times with all non-disabled students.

A description of how the student's progress will be measured and how the parents will be informed of the progress:
The teacher will assess Jacqueline informally and formally in class. A progress report will be sent home bi-weekly that states

(1) Any objectives Jacqueline mastered during this time frame

(2) Assignments either not completed or which were not acceptable and still need work

(3) Grades from any quizzes or exams taken.

(Continued)

The special educator assigned to Jacqueline will formally evaluate her mathematics progress (based on written objectives and goals) every six months, and the results will be shared with parents, her mathematics teacher, and Jacqueline. In addition, Jacqueline will be assessed for progress on all goals and objectives as well as eligibility for IDEA services.

The extent of modifications of participation in state and districtwide tests: Jacqueline will be provided with an adult who will read all tests/quizzes, and state and districtwide tests to her in an environment separate from her classroom. She will also be provided with extended time (as much time as necessary to complete the task) on these assessments.

The dates and location of services to be provided: These services are to be provided for Jacqueline in her regular education classroom from 9/7/01–9/6/02.

It is important for a teacher to have a clear understanding of her responsibility regarding her student's IEP. Figure 1.1 provides an example of critical information to be identified for each student with a disability. This form focuses specifically on mathematics, since the focus of this book is mathematics; however, it may be adapted and used for any content area. If the needed information is not found on the IEP form, it is important to request the information from the special education team.

How is a student identified as requiring special education services?

The regular education teacher's responsibility typically lies at the beginning of this process, in the referral stage, in the development of the IEP, and when services are provided. Often the regular education teacher is the first individual, other than a parent, to notice a learning problem. It is also important for the regular education teacher to be involved in the development of the IEP, if possible. The teacher is an essential component in the development of the IEP because he may provide information about how the student responds in the classroom on a daily basis to specific content and socially with other students as well as the teacher. Finally, in providing the services, the classroom teacher is responsible for instruction, working with the special education instructor to address the needs of the student. From first concerns to IEP, the process moves through the following stages.

• *The student is identified as possibly needing special-education services.* This is commonly referred to as a referral or request for evaluation. A student may be having difficulty achieving in a specific area, and a teacher or member of the school faculty may request that the student be evaluated to determine whether he has a disability in order to receive special services. Parent consent must be provided before a student is evaluated, and the evaluation needs to be completed within a reasonable amount of time after the parent or guardian gives consent.

• *The student is evaluated.* A comprehensive evaluation must be completed in all areas related to the student's possible disability. If the parents disagree with the evaluation, they have the right to take their child for an independent evaluation and the school system must pay for it.

• *Eligibility for services is determined.* A group of professionals, typically including the special education teacher, parents, classroom teachers, school psychologists, and other related professionals, determines if the student fits into one of the categories described by IDEA. The parents have a right to challenge this decision.

• *Student is found eligible for services.* Once a student is determined to be eligible for services under IDEA, the school has 30 days to write an Individualized Education Plan (IEP) for the student.

• *IEP meeting is scheduled.* To be in compliance, the school must notify all members of the meeting (this may include all members of the IEP development team), including the parents, giving enough notice so that they may attend at a time and place agreeable to parents and the school. In addition to informing the parents of the time, place, and purpose, parents must be told who will be in attendance and be allowed to invite individuals who have special expertise or knowledge of their child.

• *IEP meeting is held and the IEP is written.* The IEP team discusses the student, and writes an IEP soon after. The student may be present for this meeting, if appropriate. After the plan is written, the parents must provide their consent for the child to receive services. Parents have the right, if they do not agree with the IEP, to ask for mediation from their state education agency.

• *Services are provided.* Parents, teachers, and other service providers are given a copy of the IEP, and its services are carried out as described by the plan. Typically, students are then evaluated on an ongoing manner according to the specifics of the IEP. A complete yearly review is performed, and at least once every three years, the student is re-evaluated to determine eligibility for IDEA services.

What if a student is determined not to have
a disability and cannot receive special services?

Once a determination has been made that a student cannot receive services under IDEA, Section 504, or ADA, the classroom teacher must then meet the needs of the student without external support. It is quite common for students to exhibit difficulties consistent with students with disabilities and not qualify for services. These students can benefit from the same assessments and strategies used to bolster special learners, easing the frustrations of teachers, students, and their families. While the following chapters will discuss characteristics of students with learning disabilities and difficulties, and strategies to teach these students, many of these strategies may be useful to under-achieving students who do not qualify for special-education assistance; they may also be useful for the general population of learners. All students with difficulties learning do not have the same needs or approaches to learning. The classroom teacher assesses and evaluates her students, and she can then match strategies to specific needs.

PARAPROFESSIONALS

Particularly in the inclusive environments, many classroom teachers have a paraprofessional in the classroom. Paraprofessionals are also known as paraeducators, teachers' aides, or instructional aids, among other terms; these staff people are hired to support instruction, working alongside the teacher in the classroom in a variety of capacities. The manner in which a paraprofessional is utilized in the classroom depends upon the school and the teacher. When IDEA was amended in 1997, the responsibilities of paraprofessionals changed; they are now allowed to provide instructional assistance in special education programs if they are appropriately trained and supported.

Typically paraprofessionals serve as liaisons between regular education and special education. They spend most of their time working with small groups of students, or individuals (French, 1998). Some of their responsibilities are to tend to student's health care needs, assist students in completing assignments, instruct students one-on-one, and assist in entire general education classes where students with disabilities are included. Paraprofessionals are employed in special education primarily to increase the instructional quality and time for students with disabilities.

According to French (2002), the paraprofessional changes the role of the teacher, requires a clear delineation of roles and responsibilities, and generally lacks special training. Most teachers are not provided with training on how to supervise a paraprofessional. This can be challenging for the veteran teacher with twenty years' experience who is uncertain about having another individual in the classroom, as well as for the first-year teacher who is faced with new-teacher demands as well as having to plan and supervise another (likely older) individual in the classroom. The lead teacher now must plan instruction and make provisions for how to utilize a paraprofessional efficiently.

Paraprofessionals need their roles and responsibilities to be clearly articulated. It's best not to assume that an aide has the same knowledge base as a teacher. For example, many of these people have not had the training in teacher education that teachers have, and therefore they need many rules and other school information explicitly explained to them: school rules, policies of dealing with parents—much of the information that teacher training programs offer that a non-teacher would likely not know about. In addition, all expectations will need to be clearly delineated—what the teacher's aide can expect from the special education students, as well what will be expected of the aide as he or she works with them. Finally, paraprofessionals must become familiar with education plans of all students that they interact with.

The Paraprofessional in the Mathematics Education Classroom

Depending on the comfort level of the teacher, and the paraprofessionals' comfort level and knowledge base of mathematics and willingness to instruct, there are a variety of roles they may take on in the regular classroom. One possibility is that the paraprofessional plays an active role in planning and implementing instruction; this usually requires the teacher and paraprofessional to have common planning time. Another configuration is one in which the teacher provides instruction to the class, and the paraprofessional supports the instruction of all students who are having difficulties learning the material. At the other end of the spectrum, the paraprofessional could be utilized to independently work with only those students who are to be provided with special education services.

CONCLUSION

Currently, regular classrooms contain a larger diversity of learners than ever before. New reform movements in mathematics and trends in special education have spurred the increased inclusion of students with learning difficulties in the classroom and made it incumbent upon the regular classroom teacher to meet the needs of all students. Understanding the identification process and legal aspects of educating students with learning disabilities is the first step in the process. These will be addressed more fully in the next chapter.

Characteristics of Students with Learning Disabilities and the Impact on Learning Mathematics

2

A typical elementary teacher is required to teach many content-area subjects daily to a classroom of students with a wide range of abilities. These teachers are expected to have expertise in a variety of content areas, and to be able to teach all learners. Add to this the increasing numbers of students with disabilities in the regular classroom, and the already enormously challenging profession of teaching has been compounded. It is helpful for the teacher, in aiming to meet the additional demands of inclusion, to understand the attributes of these special needs students. Instruction may need to be adapted, modified, or various other accommodations may have to be made, based on these attributes, to facilitate success for all students.

This chapter will answer questions such as, What is a learning disability (LD)? What are the characteristics of students with learning disabilities? How do these characteristics manifest themselves when students are learning mathematics? How can these impact a student's ability to learn mathematics?

With these understandings in place, the teacher can then choose from the strategies offered throughout this book.

CHARACTERISTICS OF STUDENTS WITH LEARNING DISABILITIES

The term "specific learning disability," usually shortened to "learning disability," or LD, refers to a disorder in one or more of the basic psychological processes involved in understanding or in using language (spoken or written), which can manifest in an imperfect ability to listen, speak, read, write, spell, or to do mathematical calculations. The term includes such conditions as perceptual handicaps, brain injury, minimal brain dysfunction, dyslexia, and developmental aphasia—technical terms that are defined in the glossary at the end of this book. Under law, the term does not include children who have learning disabilities that are primarily the result of visual, hearing, or motor handicaps, nor does it include those with mental retardation, emotional disturbance, or with environmental, cultural, or economic disadvantages (U.S. Office of Education, 1977).

Children with learning disabilities fall across a spectrum. All students are unique and have their own defining characteristics. When planning instruction for any student, a teacher must look at the student's strengths and weaknesses. Similarly, when planning instruction to include a student with a disability, it helps to have an understanding of the student's attributes that challenge or interfere with learning. There are several general characteristics that many of these students possess, of which teachers should be aware prior to planning instruction. Many students with learning disabilities have some of the following characteristics:

- Information processing
  - Visual deficits
  - Auditory-processing difficulties
  - Motor disabilities
  - Memory deficiencies
  - Attention deficits
- Language
  - Expressive difficulties
  - Receptive difficulties
- Cognitive and metacognitive issues
- Difficulty maintaining positive attitudes toward learning mathematics

Figure 2.1   An Information-processing Model for Memory

Information Processing

There are several components to the information-processing model and places within the process where students may encounter difficulties when learning. The information-processing model shown in Figure 2.1 is an attempt to describe how sensory input is perceived, transformed, reduced, elaborated, stored, retrieved, and used (Swanson, 1987). Students with learning disabilities regularly demonstrate information processing difficulties that may interfere with being successful mathematics learners.

The model above describes a complicated process, much of which takes place for all of us unconsciously and automatically. A primary focus of this model is on memory (the storage and retrieval of information). The first step in learning and remembering information is to receive the information through senses or sensory receptors. Next, the information is transported to the sensory store, which holds all incoming information for approximately one second, just long enough for us to attend and perceive it. In the sensory store, both the visual representation and auditory representation are stored.

Once the information is perceived, it can be held in the short-term (working) memory, which is able to hold about seven pieces of information at one time. If the information is to be learned, it will either be transferred to and stored in long-term memory, or a strategy will be utilized to keep the information in short-term memory. Unless a strategy is used to remember this information, it will be lost in about 15 seconds. Some strategies that can be utilized to keep this information active in short-term memory are to rehearse the information, chunk it, elaborate on it, or create visual images of it. Information is then transferred from the short-term memory to long term memory where it is stored until needed.

Ease of retrieval of information is based on how it is stored in long-term memory. When retrieved for use, information from the long-term memory is transferred into short-term memory, at which point it is readily available. If it is stored meaningfully, such as by tying new information to previously stored information, retrieval will be easier. Throughout this process, the executive functioning related to planning, organizing, and strategizing behaviors, coordinates and controls learning (Bos & Vaughn, 1994).

From this theory, the importance of using strategies to move information into long-term memory in a meaningful way becomes crucial. Some strategies for instruction include the following:

- Provide cues so students are aware of important tasks or features of the task. For example, provide an overview of the lesson; write important concepts or ideas on the board or overhead.
- Teach students to use memory strategies such as mnemonics.
- Use organizational strategies such as concept maps to help organize their thinking and tie new information to previously stored information.
- Teach students to become flexible thinkers and problem-solving strategists.

Some of the difficulties related to and affecting information processing are listed below (Bley & Thornton, 1995; Mercer & Mercer, 1998):

- Visual deficits (Garnett, 1992)
- Auditory-processing difficulties (Smith, 1994)
- Motor disabilities (Smith, 1994)
- Memory deficiencies (Bos & Vaughn, 1994)
- Attention deficits (Zentall & Ferkis, 1993)

Weaknesses in any of these components of information processing may affect math performance in the following ways.

Visual Processing

Jason typically has difficulties when asked to read out loud. He often loses his place in the text, and will combine unrelated parts of sentences as a result. Each morning in mathematics class, students are required to write down the problem of the day in their notebooks and solve the problem. Jason frequently copies the problem incorrectly from the board by reversing the digits. He also has difficulties taking quizzes and tests. He often uses information from one problem coupled with information from another problem on the same page to answer a question. When setting up a number problem, he will often misalign numbers, causing his computation to be incorrect.

A visual-processing or perceptual disorder refers to a hindered ability to make sense of information taken in through the eyes. This does not include difficulties seeing or any difficulty related to the actual functioning of the eye, but refers to problems in the processing of visual information by the brain. Difficulties with visual processing affect how visual information is interpreted or processed. Types of visual-processing deficits affecting performance in mathematics include spatial perception, reversals, and figure-ground discrimination (Bley & Thornton, 1995).

The term *spatial perception* refers to the ability to accurately perceive objects in space with reference to other objects. It is the ability to discriminate right from left, top from bottom, and so on. Students with visual-spatial difficulties typically will lose their place on a worksheet or when reading a text. Spatial challenges may hinder a student's ability to write in a straight line across the paper. They may also impact the directional aspects of mathematics such as the ability to solve problems involving single-digit addition (up-down), regrouping (left-right), the alignment of numbers, or using a number line (Miller & Mercer, 1997). In addition, students with spatial-perception problems may have trouble with the concept of fractions as well as writing them, writing decimals, and find it hard to discern differences in size or shape.

Reversals are also common in students with perceptual deficiencies. There are two types of reversals, one in which a student reverses digits, creating a mirror image of a single digit, and the second when a student reverses the digits of a two-digit number. This can cause problems with regrouping and transposing digits.

Figure ground is the ability to identify an object from a background of other objects. Students with figure-ground difficulties typically lose their place on a page, mix up parts of different problems, and have difficulty reading a calculator, reading multi-digit numbers, and copying symbols incorrectly.

Visual discrimination is the ability to discern similarities and differences when comparing letters, numbers, and other objects. This includes distinguishing among common objects and symbols, color, form, shape, pattern, size, and position, as well as the ability to recognize an object as distinct from its surrounding environment. Difficulties in this area can cause students to have trouble identifying symbols, gaining information from pictures, charts, or graphs, or being able to use visually presented material in a productive way. Students with these difficulties may have trouble reading texts, worksheets, papers, or tests with too much information on one page. A student with discrimination issues may not be able to tell the difference between a quarter and a nickel, the numbers 6 and 9, and the small hand on a clock and the large one. These issues can result in interference with many mathematics skills such as measurement, estimation, problem solving, and geometry.

Auditory Processing

Thomas often has difficulty paying attention in class. He has difficulty hearing the teacher when other students are shuffling their papers, opening their desks, and preparing for the next class. When mathematics problems are dictated in class, he will almost always write down an incorrect number if it sounds like another. He has trouble deciphering numbers when he hears them; often he cannot distinguish between the numbers 30 and 13. In addition, he almost never remembers an assignment that has been orally told to him in class. However, Thomas can and does complete assignments when they are written out for him on paper or on the board.

Auditory processing refers to an individual's ability to analyze, interpret, and process information obtained through the ear. It does not apply to what is received by the eardrum, or to deafness, or being hard of hearing. Students like Thomas who have auditory-processing difficulties have problems with figure ground and discrimination. These are exhibited by Thomas' difficulty making out the teacher's voice against the background noise from other students and his difficulty discriminating between sounds of spoken numbers in class.

These students may exhibit several difficulties when learning mathematics. For example, figure-ground deficits can impede students' ability to hear a pattern in counting, and their ability to be attentive in the classroom. They have difficulties sorting out auditory information such as students and teachers talking, books shuffling, desks opening, and even the sound of chalk being used to write on the board. Auditory discrimination deficits interfere with a student's ability to decipher numbers that are spoken, such as 30 and 13 in Thomas's case—which can in turn cause problems with the student's ability to count, and to "count on" in a sequence. They may have similar difficulties with decimal numbers. Oral drills are also challenging for these students. Students with auditory deficits tend to have difficulties with using ordinal numbers (Bley & Thornton, 1995; Miller & Mercer, 1997).

Motor Disabilities

Amy is a lively third-grade student who cannot legibly write her numbers. She writes very slowly and inaccurately. Amy's numbers are very large and she cannot fit them in a typical box on a given test or quiz in her classroom. Her work often looks sloppy, as if it was completed quickly and without much effort. However, this is not the case. Amy works diligently to complete all of her mathematics assignments. As a result of her difficulties writing, she spends much more time than most of her peers do to complete her daily assignments. Amy's inability to write clearly interferes with her accuracy, and so her written work may not reflect her understanding.

It also interferes with the teacher's ability to read and appropriately evaluate what she really knows about mathematics.

Motor skill deficiencies interfere with the ability to use and coordinate large and small body muscles in order to move and manipulate objects. Many motor skill disorders are not associated with brain damage or cerebral palsy, but are often evident in children with other developmental disorders, e.g., mental retardation and autism (Smith, 1994).

Typically, this type of disability shows itself when students write letters and numbers illegibly, slowly, and inaccurately. These students usually will have difficulties writing in small spaces because they tend to write rather large. They are frequently fatigued after writing. They will often have difficulties cutting and pasting. In addition, pace, neatness, and copying will also be problematic (Wood, 1998). It is often difficult to discern just what students with motor disabilities *do* know about mathematics, as their written work can be illegible. However, the teacher must *not* infer that a messy paper indicates that the student does not know his or her mathematics.

Memory Problems

Susan's fifth-grade teacher, Mrs. Brooks, is very frustrated with her performance in mathematics and in other subjects as well. Mrs. Brooks has noticed that when she works with Susan on various topics one-on-one, she seems to grasp the material. However, this is not reflected in her homework. Although Susan appears to know, understand, and can complete work on a particular concept when she leaves the mathematics class, she returns the next day seemingly unaware that she was ever introduced to the material. Susan has trouble with long division, and can never remember the correct order of operations when solving equations. Susan often does well on daily quizzes, but has difficulty passing chapter exams containing this material.

Students with memory deficits typically have difficulty remembering information. Such students may

- understand new information in class, but be uncertain how to proceed once they leave class
- have difficulties placing information in short-term memory and thus have problems later retrieving it from long-term memory
- not easily retrieve needed information from long-term memory
- be unable to retain mathematics facts or new information readily
- forget steps in algorithms such as long division, and have a hard time when solving multi-step word problems

Difficulties remembering information may also contribute to students performing poorly when reviewing past material, and when asked to complete a variety of problems on several different concepts. In addition, these students frequently have difficulties in matters related to time (Bley & Thornton, 1995; Miller & Mercer, 1997).

Attention Deficits

Marie understands she has attention difficulties. She often finds herself in mathematics class, as well as other classes, unable to remain focused. Her teacher is very aware that Marie is not paying attention, and will frequently call out her name to redirect her attention back to mathematics. This negative attention in front of the whole class embarrasses Marie almost to tears. At other times, she will blurt out answers or ask inappropriate questions. Once she realizes that she has behaved inappropriately, Marie is very embarrassed. She is always disorganized, her locker is a mess, and she can never locate her homework (if it is done) or her daily assignment book. One a typical day, Marie will forget to take her Ritalin on time (coincidentally, an hour before mathematics class), and thus does not receive the maximum benefit from her medication.

Students such as Marie with AD/HD generally have difficulty maintaining their concentration on a topic. Although many people refer to attention-deficit/hyperactivity disorder as ADD, throughout this book the disorder will be called by its medically correct name, AD/HD.

AD/HD is one of the most commonly diagnosed behavioral disorders of childhood. The disorder is estimated to affect between 3 and 7 of every 100 school-aged children (American Psychiatric Association [APA], 2000). According to data provided by the U.S. Drug Enforcement Agency (2002), other studies have documented an even higher prevalence rate. The Mayo Clinic, in studying almost 9,000 children over a seven-year time period, documented a prevalence rate of 7.5% (Leibson, Katusic, Barbaresi, Ransom, & O'Brien, 2001).

Typical symptoms of AD/HD involve developmentally inappropriate levels of attention, hyperactivity, and impulsivity. These problems are persistent and usually cause difficulties in one or more major life areas: home, school, or social relationships. Because the disorder varies among individuals, children with AD/HD won't all have the same problems, which range from hyperactivity in some children to underactivity in others. Some may have great problems with attention. Others may be mildly inattentive but overly impulsive. Still others may have significant problems in all three areas (attention, hyperactivity, and impulsivity). The following are three subtypes of AD/HD:

- Predominantly Inattentive
- Predominantly Hyperactive-Impulsive
- Combined (inattention, hyperactivity-impulsivity)

AD/HD is characterized by serious and persistent difficulties in attention span, impulse control, and sometimes hyperactivity. In the classroom, inattention and impulsiveness are evidenced by not sticking with tasks sufficiently to finish them, and by having difficulty organizing and completing work correctly. Often, students may actually be attending to too many things at once. The student may give the impression that he or she is not listening or has not heard what has been said. The student's work is often messy and performed carelessly and impulsively. In a mathematics classroom, an AD/HD student can have difficulties maintaining attention to steps in algorithms or problem solving as well as to essential instruction. In addition, there are many other students who have difficulties maintaining attention to the task at hand who do not have this diagnosis, but may benefit from strategies offered for this disability in Chapter 3.

Often, students with AD/HD are treated with drugs such as Ritalin in order to help them focus better. The timing as well as dosage of the drug is critical; as the amount in the student's system can dramatically change during the day. It is critical that the teacher be aware of the medication needs of a student, both when and how much the student is currently taking. However, not all students with this disorder take this drug. AD/HD is a controversial topic, both for usage of Ritalin and because some believe that AD/HD is the result of environmental conditions.

Language Disabilities

Albert has trouble when he is asked to verbally state how he would solve a problem; however, he does not have problems *writing out* how he solved the problem. He is often confused by new vocabulary when reading a section of his mathematics book. He also frequently has problems when reading a word or story problem, and therefore cannot complete the problem. Because he frequently has trouble with new vocabulary, he is very reticent about participating and is often very quiet in class.

Expressive Difficulties

Many students with learning disabilities have difficulties with expressive and/or receptive language processing. Expressive language issues impact a student's ability to complete such tasks as rapid oral drills, counting on, and explaining verbally why a problem is solved in a certain manner. The ability to communicate about mathematics both in writing and verbally is beneficial for students as they strive to develop their own more complex understandings. In addition, it is important for the teacher to be able to identify students' mathematical understandings and misunderstandings to further their mathematical development.

Receptive Difficulties

Receptive language difficulties manifest themselves with a student having difficulties relating words to meaning; for example, connecting vocabulary words with an understanding of mathematical concepts such as first and greater than. These students will often have difficulties with words that have multiple meanings (sum, times, difference) and also with writing numbers from dictation. In addition, they may have trouble following directions and solving word problems (Bley & Thornton, 1995). Often, lack of comprehension of mathematical vocabulary impedes these students' ability to read a mathematics textbook or word problem (Smith, 1994). Mathematical symbols represent a way to express numerical language concepts, and thus language skills become very important to calculations, word problems, and ultimately to mathematical achievement.

Irrelevant numerical and linguistic information in word problems is especially troublesome for many students with learning disabilities (Englert, Culatta, & Horn, 1987). Students can become confused if irrelevant information is included in a word problem. For example, in the following problem: Stacey drove down Highway 95 for 20 minutes at 55 mph. How many miles did she travel? A student with a language deficit may become confused by the number 95, not realizing that it is extraneous information, irrelevant to solving the problem. Since teachers frequently evaluate students by asking them to explain their thinking either verbally or in written form, it can be very difficult to determine what a student knows who has an expressive and/or receptive language deficit.

Cognitive and Metacognitive Issues

Dan often seems lost when it comes to mathematics. In class, it appears as if he is just guessing about how to set up and solve word problems and how to complete the computations involved. In an attempt to learn about Dan's understanding of mathematics, his teacher has discovered that he frequently cannot select an appropriate strategy to solve a problem. In fact, for the most part, he does not seem have a specific approach for solving mathematics problems. At times, Dan can demonstrate that he understands a concept. However, when multiple concepts are involved such as subtraction, multiplication, addition, and division, he will often have difficulty correctly solving the problems.

Cognition as it refers to "understanding" is the ability to comprehend what you see and hear, and to infer information from social cues and body language. Metacognition emphasizes self-awareness of how one approaches a task in order to plan and monitor progress. It is sometimes described as "thinking about your thinking." Students who have deficiencies in these areas commonly lack awareness of basic skills, strategies, and resources necessary to complete mathematics tasks. Trouble selecting appropriate strategies to solve problems, along with the lack of self-regulatory mechanisms to work problems through, further complicate their success in problem solving (Brownell, Mellard, & Deshler, 1993; Mercer, 1997). Specifically, these students have difficulty in the following areas:

- assessing their abilities to solve problems
- identifying and selecting appropriate strategies
- organizing information
- monitoring problem-solving processes
- evaluating problems for accuracy
- generalizing strategies to new situations

Making students consciously aware of these processes and helping them to acquire and use them is a lifelong gift that a teacher can give.

MAINTAINING POSITIVE ATTITUDES TOWARD LEARNING MATHEMATICS

On a typical day, Tony will do anything to get out of mathematics class. Tony holds the belief that he will never be good at mathematics because he has never been good at mathematics. He has had failure throughout his years of schooling in mathematics. Tony tends to act flustered and tense when faced with the task of "doing mathematics." In recent weeks, his behavior has become more disruptive than usual; almost immediately preceding mathematics class, he acts out inappropriately and is usually sent out of class or given a time-out. His teacher believes that he is trying to avoid the class.

Both curriculum design and teacher behavior directly influence the mathematics achievement of students with learning difficulties (Mercer, Jordan, & Miller, 1996). Success in solving mathematics problems is not based solely on one's knowledge of mathematics. It is also based on metacognitive processes related to mathematics strategy usage, the emotions an individual feels when doing a problem, and the personal beliefs about one's mathematical abilities (Garofalo & Lester, 1985; McLeod, 1988; Schoenfeld, 1985). Thus, it is essential to have a thorough understanding of your students, their special needs, and their relationship to the curriculum. Equally significant is instilling the belief in your students that they can and will be successful at learning important mathematics concepts. Responding to a student in a manner that promotes student thinking and encourages students to take risks is vital for the development of persistence and ownership of mathematics.

While many students have problems maintaining positive attitudes toward mathematics, we also know that negative attitudes can promote a lack of persistence in learning mathematics. Many students with disabilities have histories of academic failure that contribute to the development of learned helplessness in math (Parmar & Cawley, 1991). Poor academic self-concept, low self-esteem, negative attitudes, or teachers' erroneous perceptions of students with learning disabilities may be associated with their poor academic and social outcomes (Montague, 1997).

Many special education students have holes in their mathematics background as well as in their conceptual understandings. Often, these result in the students' development of misunderstandings about mathematics and negative dispositions toward their own mathematical abilities. The National Council for Teaching Mathematics (NCTM, 2000) states that developing a positive attitude toward learning mathematics is an important aspect of a student's learning experience. Many studies have shown the importance of attitude to success in mathematics.

The issue of maintaining a positive attitude toward mathematics is not solely a problem for learning-disabled students; it is also a problem for the general population (Sliva & Roddick, 2001). Further, and not surprisingly, evidence points to the idea that repeated failure and negative interactions place students at great risk for experiencing negative affect (Yasutake & Bryant, 1995). Negative affect translates into poor academic self-concept, low expectations of future academic performance, attribution of failure to low ability, and attribution of success to external factors, all of which are characteristic of students with learning disabilities (Licht, 1993). These students experience social difficulties, have low self-esteem, and are often perceived by their teachers as being less socially competent than higher achieving students (Haager & Vaughn, 1995). In contrast, students who base their successes on hard work, and who have positive self-perceptions, generally try harder and persist longer at challenging tasks (Licht & Dweck, 1984). Thus, when teaching mathematics, it is important to be cognizant of the affective domain. Empowering students by providing them with opportunities to share what they know is one approach to facilitate this process. Others will be discussed in Chapter 3.

CONCLUSION

Awareness of difficulties that learning-disabled students face can enable teachers to open their eyes more to the experience that these children have while trying to learn mathematics. Not every classroom teacher needs to be a diagnostician, but most will feel more prepared to help their students when they know that a messy paper does not necessarily indicate sloppiness and forgetting an assignment is not always carelessness. In the next chapter, strategies are offered for teachers to include these students more fully and successfully in the learning taking place in the classroom.

In this chapter we have looked closely at aspects of learning that provide strategic intervention points for helping students, including the following:

- Information processing
  - Visual deficits
  - Auditory-processing difficulties
  - Motor disabilities
  - Memory deficiencies
  - Attention deficits
- Language
  - Expressive difficulties
  - Receptive difficulties
- Cognitive and metacognitive issues
- Difficulty maintaining positive attitudes toward learning mathematics

In the next chapter, we will look at strategies that can be targeted to these areas of challenge.

Specific 3 Strategies for Instruction

For people to participate fully in society, they must know basic mathematics. Citizens who cannot reason mathematically are cut off from whole realms of human endeavor.

—National Research Council (2001, p. 1)

This quote is a reminder of how important mathematics is to all people in society. In the past, it seemed as if "geniuses" were the only ones able to "do" mathematics (Mtetwa & Garofalo, 1989). However, this is not the case, and all students—even students with learning difficulties—can learn mathematics. This chapter will discuss specific instructional strategies and modification that can help to address each of the characteristics of students with learning disabilities discussed in Chapter 2. Although the strategies and modifications are each tailored to a specific deficit, many of these can enhance the learning of all students. The teacher can explicitly help learning-disabled students become aware of compensatory strategies that they can use and practice to complete the tasks in class and to learn more mathematics, and these can be carried by the students into their other learning experiences and their lives to help them to become life-long learners.

STRATEGIES TO FACILITATE INFORMATION PROCESSING

As described in Chapter 2, information-processing deficits impact many students with learning difficulties through challenges to multiple aspects of processing: visual, auditory, motor, memory, and attention. Strategies and modifications to include these learners in the regular education classroom are needed.

Visual-processing Strategies

Many learning-disabled students, like their non-disabled peers, are concrete in their thinking; using concrete representations such as manipulatives can help these students represent and organize their thinking. Students with visual-processing difficulties have trouble making sense of information visually. Some implications of these difficulties include losing their place on a worksheet or while reading a text; confusing unrelated information on a page; reversing digits; and the inability to differentiate objects based on their individual characteristics.

There are a variety of strategies and modifications that can be useful to help students with these difficulties. Some modifications to compensate for these deficits include the following:

- Separate problems on a worksheet, test, or text. Individual problems may be cut and pasted on single sheets of paper. It is very important to simplify tests and worksheets as much as possible so students do not confuse material on the page.
- Create a template that can be used to isolate certain problems, paragraphs, or sentences on a page. The template may be created on a computer and consistently used so that a student gets accustomed to the format of the paper. (Example: Figure 3.2)
- Highlighters can be used by students to help them emphasize important material.
- Seat students as close to the board or overhead screen as possible.
- Use larger-than-normal print size for reading material such as textbooks and worksheets. Often, special textbooks and workbooks can be ordered, or a photocopy machine may be used to enlarge print.
- When using an overhead projector with transparencies, use a large print size—at least 18 points. Limit the number of lines written and the number of problems, as well, based on this font size.
- Provide photocopies of notes written on the board or overhead projector. All photocopies should be as clear as possible. Students with visual or motor-processing difficulties may have trouble copying information from the board or overhead machine. Carbon paper used under another student's notes may also be utilized for the same purpose.

- Separate the problem number from the problem. Possibly circle the problem number, separate with parenthesis, make bold, or leave extra space after the number. For example:

  1. $3 + 5 =$ ___

  becomes

  (1) $3 + 5 =$ ___

- Provide lined or graph paper for students who have difficulties with spatial relations. Graph paper is useful to provide a structure for keeping numbers on the same line and spaced appropriately. The size of the cells on the graph will depend on the activity being completed. It may also depend on the grade level—with younger students (i.e., PreK–2), you may use larger graph blocks such as 1 cm, and use smaller ones for older students.
- Use colored chalk, overhead pens, or colored pencils to separate important aspects of a problem for a student. For example, a teacher may underline what the question is asking in blue, to set that apart from the rest of the problem. Students should also use this method in their own work, as well. Colored pens on the overhead and colored chalk on the board provide contrast, which may help to engage learners and facilitate learning for those students who have perceptual difficulties. Using separate colors to identify the needed information in a word problem from the mathematical expression of what the problem asks for may also be helpful.
- Use multi-sensory (auditory, visual, tactile [touch], and kinesthetic) approaches to learning whenever possible (e.g., use visual cueing: boxes, circles, and lines; or color code).
- Allow extra time on assessments for students who have processing difficulties.
- As much as possible, provide verbal as well as visual (written) instructions for an assignment. This can be done with weekly assignment sheets as well as written assignments on the overhead or board, or assignments can be provided on a Web site.
- Corrections to mirror image reversals can be aided by having students use stencils, and finger trace. Students can also verbalize, saying things like "Down, around, the 6 curls up; the 6 sleeps sound" as they are tracing.
- Color coding the tens (green) and ones digits (red) are useful for those students who have a problem with reversing two-digit numbers. Green can be coded for the students as the place to "start" when discussing the number. Also, prerecorded tapes (easily made by the teacher) for student use are helpful to practice writing numbers.

- Books on tape are useful for students who have visual-processing difficulties, as well as for students who have strengths in auditory processing.
- Whenever possible, use manipulatives with students who have figure-ground difficulties. For example, instead of using a worksheet with pictures of coins on it, use actual coins. This will help students to discern the shapes from the background.

In addition to these strategies, some students will have invented their own, and some may have to be created through trial and error. When teachers partner with students in this way to find successful strategies, both grow in confidence and their repertoire expands. One goal with students who have difficulties learning is to provide compensatory strategies and modifications so that they have access to learning the material.

It is necessary at first for teachers to provide the needed strategies and modifications; however, students should also be taught when to use these in the future. For example, a teacher may create a template for the student to use when reading his mathematics textbook or when doing mathematics problems, but the student needs to learn when he needs to use the template. This template may block out everything on the page except a line of text, so the student can focus on that sentence and not get lost on the page. Or a template may ask questions such as, What does the first paragraph on the page mean? What does the picture have to do with what the text is saying? It may also ask students to put in their own words what they have learned or what they are having difficulty with.

Students may also be able to tell you about successful strategies learned in other classes that can be incorporated. As they become accustomed to thinking about what helps them, they will become more independently successful in their work. Many of the above-mentioned strategies will also be useful to students without disabilities, as they often make the tasks more clear.

Auditory-processing Strategies

Auditory deficits can interfere with a student's ability to hear differences between numbers such as 40 and 14, hear patterns in numbers, and be attentive in the classroom. The following are some strategies and modifications that can be used to compensate for these deficiencies:

- Verbal directions and explanations should be simplified as much as possible and supplemented with written or other visual cues.
- Use concrete or pictorial representations of mathematics concepts.

- Students should be seated where sound is as clear as possible. Avoid seating a student near the door where hallway sound may be distracting. For independent work, provide a quiet workspace.
- The teacher should slow her rate of speech and use changes in tone and pitch to keep students interested.
- Use appropriate vocabulary. If students are unfamiliar with the vocabulary, this may compound their difficulties understanding.
- Minimize distractions.
- Allow the student to tape record a class to review later.

It can be difficult for any student to hear homework assigned quickly at the end of the class period when other students are beginning to file out of the room. It is difficult almost to the point of impossibility for students who have auditory-processing disorders. There are also many possible distractions in the room such as students closing books, putting their materials away, and beginning to get out of their seats. When giving any verbal directions, make sure that the room is quiet, and that you have students' attention. You might want to develop a consistent visual cue to alert them that important information or directions are coming. Some teachers use a raised hand as a signal for quiet and attention or flash the classroom lights to signal the students to stop what they are doing and listen. These signals work for the entire class. It may be helpful to involve special education students in choosing signals that will cue them to pay attention. Some possible signals to gain students' attention are listed below:

- Turn/flash classroom lights on/off
- Raise hand and wait for all students to raise their hands and be quiet
- Ring a bell
- Clap your hands together

Private cues to help an individual student pay attention can be established between the student and the teacher such as tapping a student's desk or shoulder. Again, it is most beneficial if the student comes up with a signal in collaboration with the teacher, as it may be more meaningful to the student.

In addition to alerting students that directions are about to be given, it is important for all students and critical for special learners that teachers provide homework or special directions in written form so that those students who have difficulties with auditory processing may receive the same information in another manner. If your classroom or school has a Web site, it is helpful to all students—and again, particularly helpful to special learners and their parents—if you use it to post assignments, information about projects, or anything that will help students access at home what they have missed at school. Finally, when presenting new information verbally, utilize concrete or pictorial representations to provide these students with visual clues.

Figure 3.1 is an example of an exam with too much information on one page. This exam has too much information close together for a student who has visual-processing problems. These students often have difficulty with spatial relations and therefore could lose their place on the page, confusing information from one problem with that of another problem. In addition, students who have AD/HD or are easily distracted may become distracted with tests that have too much information close together on a page.

Figure 3.2 provides a look at the same exam, edited. This figure demonstrates one possible way to make this test easier to follow. Four of the problems are re-done; each has extra space for the problem and is boxed off to alleviate confusion. There are reminders for each problem to show work, draw a picture, and write the answer in a complete sentence; the directions are written more clearly; and there are fewer problems per page. In addition, the information needed for problems 6 and 7 are written with the actual problem. It may be necessary to include only one or two problems per page, depending on the student. All of these modifications create fewer distractions for the student, hopefully allowing for more success.

Motor Strategies

One way deficiencies in the area of motor skills can be evidenced is by a student having difficulties writing letters and numbers. These students are often fatigued after writing and have trouble manipulating small objects, tracing, or copying. It can be difficult to determine what a student knows when discerning his writing is difficult. The following are some strategies and modifications to facilitate learning for these students:

- Orally assess the student. If a student cannot adequately write her answer, another individual (or teacher) may write down what the student requests. Computers have become useful tools for students with motor difficulties as students can type their thoughts, creating a word-processed document, which is easily read. Recently, voice-activated software such as Dragon has been developed, which can translate the student's words into a document that is, again, easily read by others.
- Provide photocopies of notes written on the board or overhead machine. Introduce copying exercises slowly, gradually adding more material to be copied each time.
- Carbon paper used under another student's notes may be utilized to provide copies of notes for the student.

Figure 3.1 Exam Sample

Example of exam prior to modifications for students with disabilities.

Name _____
Period _____
Date _____

Directions: Solve each problem. Show all of your work, draw a picture to represent your answer, and write a complete sentence that expresses your final answer.

1. Sam picked 33 apples a day for 4 days in a row. How many apples did Sam pick all together?

2. Alessandro made $15.00 a day for 3 days. How much money did Alessandro have at the end of the third day?

3. There were 32 bees in the flower garden. Farmer Jenny could catch 8 bees at a time in her net. How many times did she have to use her net to catch the bees?

4. Daniel caught 12 butterflies each day for 6 days. On the seventh day, 2 butterflies escaped. How many butterflies did he have left?

5. Arifa has 16 friends she wants to invite to her house for lunch. If each friend will eat 1 hamburger and drink 2 glasses of soda, how many hamburgers and how many sodas does she have to buy?

Use the following information for both problems 6 and 7.

Amy and Evonne are roommates and share an apartment. They have 3 monthly payments they must make: rent for the apartment is $300.00; electricity is $20.00, and their phone charges are $40.00. They each individually pay for their own food.

6. What are Amy and Evonne each paying per month to live in their apartment?

7. If a third roommate, Trisha, moves into the apartment, how much would each roommate then pay to live in the apartment?

Figure 3.2 Sample Template

Example of a template to isolate problems on a page and make expectations clear.

Name _____
Period _____
Date _____

Directions: Solve each equation.
- Show all of your work.
- Draw a picture to represent your answer.
- Write a complete sentence that expresses your final answer.

---

1. Sam picked 33 apples a day for 4 days in a row. How many apples did Sam pick all together?

   Draw a picture: **Work:**

   Answer in a complete sentence:

---

2. Alessandro made $15.00 a day for 3 days. How much money did Alessandro have at the end of the third day?

   Draw a picture: **Work:**

   Answer in a complete sentence:

(Continued)

6. Amy and Evonne are roommates and share an apartment. They have 3 monthly payments they must make: rent for the apartment is $300.00; electricity is $20.00, and their phone charges are $40.00. They each individually pay for their own food.

   What are Amy and Evonne each paying per month to live in their apartment?

   Draw a picture: **Work:**

   Answer in a complete sentence:

7. Amy and Evonne are roommates and share an apartment. They have 3 monthly payments they must make: rent for the apartment is $300.00; electricity is $20.00, and their phone charges are $40.00. They each individually pay for their own food.

   If a third roommate, Trisha, moves into the apartment, how much would each roommate then pay to live in the apartment?

   Draw a picture: **Work:**

   Answer in a complete sentence:

- Graph paper is useful to provide a structure for keeping numbers on the same line and spaced appropriately.
- Minimize the number of assigned problems that the student needs to write answers for.
- Allow the use of tape recorders or another adult to act as a scribe.
- Allow the student to utilize a tape recorder to provide reinforcement for any material missed in class.
- Utilize alternative assessments.

Often, students with motor-processing deficiencies have difficulties demonstrating what they understand; this can be frustrating for both the student and the teacher. This is one area where technology can assist students considerably. These students can more easily express their knowledge using computers, tape recorders, and various software.

Memory Strategies

Many students with learning disabilities have difficulty remembering or recalling information (Olson & Platt, 1996). In addition, they have trouble identifying relevant information within a problem and organizing the information. Research on the information-processing model (for more detail, see Chapter 2) has shown that learning is a complicated process. Problems with short-term or long-term memory may interfere with a student's ability to retain information. Mehring and Banikowski (2002) suggest the following strategies to enhance memory:

- *Attention.* Gain the students' attention.
- *Need.* Whenever learning can be connected to real life, it will be more effective.
- Help students see the relationship between the specific learning goal and personal learning goals.
- *Cues.* In order to focus attention, use cues such as turning lights on and off, walk around the room, ask questions, or call out a student's name.
- *Emotion.* Emotions chemically stimulate the brain, which helps individuals to retain information better. Therefore, information obtained through an emotional "hook" is more likely to be remembered. This may take the shape of story telling, role-playing, drawing, and creating their own problems.
- *Meaning.* The more the information learned has meaning to the student, the more likely the student is to retain the information. Generally, the more the student is actively engaged, the more meaningful the learning. Mathematical applications that have relevance to the student help them remember the information better; teaching

Figure 3.3   Topics in Mathematics and Real-life Applications.

These are examples of topics in mathematics and some real-life examples that may be referred to when teaching these concepts.

Topic	Application
Addition	adding the points up during a sports event
Subtraction	paying bills
Multiplication	finding out how many total ounces of juice are needed for six people if they each get 8 oz.
Division	sharing candy equally with friends

mathematics with real-life applications is particularly valuable to special education students. For example, when teaching about equal parts, it is important for students to use a variety of "equal parts" that are relevant to their lives, such as equal numbers of candy or pencils, equal parts of paper, or areas of a desk. Links like those in Figure 3.3 between mathematics and real life help students to connect the new knowledge (mathematics) with something with which they are already familiar.

- *Short-term Memory (STM)*. Students need to have information presented in small pieces, and the opportunity to practice what they have learned, to be appropriately processed in STM. In addition to practice, the new information should be connected to other previously known information. To keep information active in short-term memory, it should be rehearsed, chunked, and either elaborated upon or visual images should be created.
- *Long-term Memory (LTM)*. Students with mild cognitive disabilities require approximately five times as many opportunities to practice information to get it imbedded in LTM as their non-impaired peers. Depending on the type of memory recall required, facts, concepts, rules, or the ability to recall steps, different strategies are needed. Strategies mentioned below can be helpful for all students.

Methods to Enhance Memory

- Graphic organizers such as concept maps may be useful to strengthen information, organize it, tie new information to previously stored information, and move it into long-term memory. Typically, special education students need extra practice to facilitate better understanding of the concept being taught. In addition, they often need connections among mathematics topics stated explicitly to develop a cohesive understanding. For example, students need to be explicitly taught about the relationships between division and subtraction. Concept maps may be useful to help develop these connections and visually represent them as well (Baroody & Bartels, 2000). See Chapter 4 for an example.

- Provide cues so students are aware of important tasks or features of the task. For example, provide an overview of the lesson; write important concepts or ideas on the board or overhead.
- Using manipulatives to first introduce difficult concepts and to teach abstract concepts provides the students with a visual representation to tie to the concept. Students with memory difficulties typically need a considerable amount of "overlearning" before they can retain a concept (Bley & Thornton, 1995). Teaching mathematics using manipulatives facilitates the learning of students who learn best by "doing."
- Using multiple representations to teach a concept will benefit these students, as they provide a variety of ways of seeing the same concept and create more than one way for this information to enter into memory. For examples of using multiple representations, see Chapter 4.
- Mnemonics may help students remember larger amounts of information. Meaningful learning and study techniques such as mnemonic strategies can facilitate retrieval of information from LTM. For example, a teacher may introduce the mnemonic, "King Henry Died Monday Drinking Chocolate Milk." This mnemonic helps students remember the progression of the metric system: kilometer, hectometer, dekameter, meter, decimeter, centimeter, and millimeter. It is also beneficial for students to create their own mnemonics to deepen their understandings of new material.

Difficulties remembering information learned are common for many students with learning disabilities. The strategies mentioned here are designed to help students learn, retain, and recall information more easily. They are not only helpful for students with learning difficulties, but for all students.

Attention-deficit Strategies

It is challenging to deal with a classroom full of students; it is even more so when one of your students has an attention deficit (AD/HD). Communication with the school nurse, the parents, and even possibly the physician is necessary when trying to balance the dosage of Ritalin or other medication. Between 60 and 90 percent of students with AD/HD are treated with some form of medication. The teacher is generally notified if a child's parents and doctor decide that medication will be used. Often, teachers are asked to report on whether or not the child functions better in the class while on the medication. The following paragraphs present some important strategies for instruction of students with attention difficulties:

According to Zentall and Ferkis (1993), "The . . . mathematical instruction of youth with LD, ADD, and AD/HD calls for:

- mastery learning, which builds on prerequisite skills and understandings, rather than spiral learning;
- learning that involves active construction of meanings;
- verbal teacher interactions with the child to assess and simulate problem-solution strategies;
- decreased emphasis on assessment and teaching of mathematical concepts;
- use of strategies, where appropriate, related to the requirements for reading comprehension and for memory in problem solving (e.g., for multiple-step problems);
- attentional cues to help students prepare for changes in problem action, operation, and order of operation; and
- novel instructional activities to facilitate overlearning basic calculations (i.e., to increase automization)." (p.16)

Many students have difficulty paying attention in class, not just students with AD/HD. To help these students, it is often helpful to speak with them individually and determine if they are aware of having difficulties in this area. Often, students can contribute to the process of determining what strategies will work best to refocus their attention. Since no two students are alike, it is important to identify a student's strengths and weaknesses to develop a plan for instruction. This may be done through observing the student over time; speaking with the student, his parents, and previous teachers; and trying different strategies. Teachers need a repertoire of strategies for getting, focusing, and maintaining a student's attention and keeping a student on task. These students benefit from consistency, order, and being seated among students who will not distract or be distracted by them. Listed below are several suggestions for teaching students diagnosed with attention deficits.

- Place students in the front row or near the teacher's desk
- Maintain frequent eye contact with the students
- Provide clear directions both verbally and visually
- Provide a work area for the student away from distractions
- Provide clear and consistent transitions from one topic to the next

- Use color highlighting at the chalkboard and on transparencies to help attract and hold a student's attention
- Provide a structured environment with a given place for materials and books as well as structure for instruction
- Provide stimulation and variety in lessons

LANGUAGE STRATEGIES

Many students with learning disabilities have difficulties with expressive and/or receptive language processing. Expressive language issues impact a student's ability to complete such tasks as explaining why a problem is solved in a certain manner. Receptive language difficulties manifest themselves when a student has difficulties relating words to meaning, such as vocabulary words, or has trouble understanding mathematical concepts.

Strategies for teaching students with expressive language difficulties:

- Allow students to use manipulatives or pictorial representations to support their communication of knowledge.
- Require students to practice their mathematical thinking by communicating on a daily basis in a whole-class environment, in small groups, and/or with a peer or with the teacher.
- Provide extended time for written tasks.

Strategies for teaching students with receptive language difficulties:

- Pre-teach vocabulary.
- Use concrete and pictorial representations as much as possible to solidify the meaning of concepts and vocabulary.

Requiring students to create pictorial representations of vocabulary is often an effective means to facilitate student learning. For example, to help develop your students' understanding of parallel lines, you may ask them to draw a real-life representation of the concept. This lesson might produce pictures of trees, window blinds, racetracks, and some surprises. By bringing in their own experience and sharing with small groups or the whole class, they strengthen their understanding of an abstract concept. Another approach is to ask students to create their own pictorial representation of vocabulary; these pictures may often turn out to be idiosyncratic. For example, one student demonstrated his method of remembering the coordinates of the origin: He had pasted a picture of Robert Parrish (a Boston Celtics basketball player who wore the number 00) in the center of the Cartesian graph.

COGNITIVE AND METACOGNITIVE STRATEGIES

If students with cognitive and metacognitive difficulties are taught to use appropriate learning strategies like organizing information, monitoring problem-solving processes, evaluating problems for accuracy, and generalizing strategies to appropriate situations, and are reinforced for using them, they can perform effectively (Montague, Bos, & Doucette, 1991). Two strategies to help students with these difficulties learn mathematics are to model using "think aloud" and to teach metacognitive strategies.

Modeling using thinking aloud is especially important for students who have difficulty knowing when to select and use appropriate strategies. While learning a new concept or skill, it is important for students to have a model from which to work. Using overt "think-aloud" strategies, as well as having other students model or act out their problem-solving strategies, may also be helpful. Another such strategy is to ask the student to explain her thinking. Explaining and writing out problem-solving processes are useful strategies for exploring and developing a student's reasoning patterns. One approach to help these students is to require them to describe their own thought processes while completing a problem. NCTM (2000) promotes students "thinking aloud" and explaining their thinking both verbally and in written form. Writing out explicitly (and / or explaining verbally) how students solved a problem can provide a window into how they are thinking about a problem, so that you can then develop more effective strategy usage.

Figure 3.4 is an example of a "think-aloud" strategy that enables the teacher to model appropriate behaviors for problem solving. The teacher can model the process for the whole class, and then use it individually with struggling students to both scaffold and access them while the rest of the class is working independently. The discussion between Colin, a first-grade student who is having difficulties in mathematics, and his teacher focuses on his completion of a word problem involving addition. All teachers can benefit from using this strategy because it will help them learn about the thought processes of their students.

Finally, the teacher would ask Colin to review how he solved the problem. The teacher should be careful to make sure Colin is saying what he would to do to solve the problem and not just repeating what the problem says. Then Colin should try another similar problem and verbalize his process for solving it. This process can vary depending on the student.

Explicitly teach your students learning strategies. Many of those strategies are evident in the "think aloud" suggestions just mentioned. However, helping students name and make these skills their own requires explicit teaching, and again, this will benefit many members of the class

Figure 3.4   Example of a Think Aloud

This is an example of a Think Aloud that enables the teacher to model appropriate behaviors for problem solving.

Teacher: OK, Colin, if I were going to solve this problem I will first have to read it and make sure I know what the problem is asking and what they are looking for in an answer. Let me show you how I would solve this problem. I would read the problem like this: "On a warm summer day, there were 14 ladybugs in the tree. When the wind blew, 4 more ladybugs from a flower flew over to the tree and joined them. How many total ladybugs are now in the tree?" You don't have to read it aloud as I did, but you should read it to yourself. Do you know what I mean by read it to yourself, Colin?

Colin: Is that like reading the words in my head but not saying them?

Teacher: Yes, Colin, that is like reading the words in your head but not saying them. Is it easier if you read aloud? Do you understand more of what you read if you read aloud? (The teacher is attempting to learn more about how Colin thinks, as well as trying to help him understand more about himself and how he learns best).

Colin: Yes, I understand more if I read aloud.

Teacher: OK. Then you should read the problem out loud so that you can help yourself learn more easily. Now, after I have read the problem, I ask myself, "Do I understand what the problem says?" And then I try to think in my head, What does the problem say? So for instance, I might say to myself that the problem says there are 14 ladybugs and 4 more came over. How many ladybugs are there? I believe I understand the problem. If I cannot put the problem in my own words, I think I may not be able to solve it.

Colin: So I need to use my own words, not just say what the problem says?

Teacher: Yes, it is important for you to put the problem into your own words rather than just read it again, because it lets you know if you really understand the problem.

Colin: OK. You mean if I can read a problem, it doesn't mean I know how to solve it?

Teacher: You are exactly right! Let's continue. OK. So I have read the problem, I know what it means, so now I have to figure out what they want me to answer or solve for.

Colin: They want to know how many total ladybugs!

Teacher: That's correct. So, now I want to know, How can I solve this? Have you ever worked with blocks in mathematics class before, Colin?

Colin: Yes. Last year we used to count them and other things.

Teacher: Can we pretend that blocks are ladybugs?

(Continued)

Figure 3.4 (Continued)

Colin:	Yes, let me get some. (Colin goes to the back of the room and gathers a bucket of blocks.)
Teacher:	Great. OK, so how can we do this? I am going to go back to the problem, and it says I have 14 ladybugs in a tree.
Colin:	So we need 14 ladybugs; I will get 14 blocks. (Colin counts out 14 blocks.) Ok, ready.
Teacher:	Excellent. Again I am going to go back to the problem and see that 4 more ladybugs flew over to the tree.
Colin:	(Interrupts) I need 4 more ladybugs or blocks. (He counts them out and adds to the group of blocks he previously counted.) OK, I have 18 blocks.
Teacher:	Very good. But why do you have 18 blocks?
Colin:	Because I had 14 and then I added 4 more and that makes 18.
Teacher:	Why did you add them together?
Colin:	Because when I made the problem in my own words, I knew it meant to add them.
Teacher:	So what is your answer?
Colin:	18 ladybugs.
Teacher:	Very good! Now let's review how we solved this problem.

beyond those identified with learning disabilities. Students with metacognitive difficulties can become more aware of their own thinking by practicing and developing the following skills:

- Identifying and selecting appropriate strategies. To help with this, a teacher may want to ask the student if she can think of a problem that is similar and remember how she solved that problem.
- Organizing information. The teacher may want to discuss with the student such strategies as making a table or graphically representing data.
- Monitoring problem-solving processes. Brainstorm the elements of problem solving with students, and help them learn ways to remember these components.
- Evaluating problems for accuracy. This may include helping students with different estimation strategies, as well as suggesting possible methods for checking student work.
- Generalizing strategies to appropriate situations. To help the student, the teacher may want to work with him to generate a list of strategies to solve similar problems.

STRATEGIES FOR PROMOTING A POSITIVE ATTITUDE TOWARD MATHEMATICS

Many students with learning disabilities have poor self-concept regarding their mathematical abilities. Some tools to use when assessing a student's attitude toward learning mathematics include the following:

- Mathematics autobiographies (verbal and written)
- Journal writing
- Inventories
- Interviews

Mathematics Autobiographies

To obtain information about a student's experience and attitude learning mathematics, a teacher may use a "Mathematics Autobiography." A mathematics autobiography is a student's description of his feelings about mathematics, in his own words. If a student is very young, the prompts may be asked verbally and the answers recorded by a teacher or parent. Otherwise, students can write down their answers or record them using a tape recorder. The questions that are asked of the student can vary, but here are some suggestions to include:

- What experiences do you remember about learning mathematics?
- What is your favorite/least favorite part of learning mathematics?
- Do you see mathematics as being part of your daily life?

After a student has answered these questions, the teacher may want to ask further questions for clarification, to fully understand the student's intentions. This may also be done verbally in the form of an interview, for those students who may be younger or have difficulties writing.

After initially assessing attitude via the mathematics autobiography, instruction can then be tailored to address the issues mentioned and work to improve attitude. For instance, if a student mentions enjoying learning using blocks and "hands-on" activities, and not enjoying learning just from lecture, a teacher may want to make sure that a large portion of the instruction given to this student is hands-on. Another comment that students frequently make is that they do not like to be called on in class. We want students to be able to express their ideas mathematically; this is an important component of learning mathematics. Therefore, a teacher may want to speak to the student and explain why he/she would call on the student in class, and delve more deeply into why the student does not want to respond in class. One approach is to make sure that a student feels comfortable in the class before calling on the student. Perhaps the teacher can find a way to make sure that when a student is initially called on, early in the year, that he/she will give the correct answer. Again, this approach to assessing a student's past experiences in mathematics is beneficial for all students, not just those who are learning disabled.

Journals

There are several ways in which journals can be used in the mathematics classroom, one of which is as a means to assess and evaluate a student's attitude toward learning mathematics. Students may be asked to write about their attitudes and feelings toward mathematics. The following is a list of helpful tips for managing mathematical journals:

1. Provide students with thin, inexpensive journals, which can be added on to as the year progresses.

2. Store journals in one consistent place in the classroom.

3. Determine a system for identifying journal entries (e.g., have students number the entries or date them).

4. Establish a system for collecting and distributing the journals.

5. Set aside a time for writing in journals (Baxter, Woodward, Olson, & Robyns, 2002).

If students have not used mathematics journals previously, a teacher may want to start with more structured questions for journal prompts. For example:

Today in class I enjoyed _____ the most.

I discovered _____ .

As the year progresses, more advanced and open-ended prompts may be used such as

How do you feel when you have completed your homework?

How do you complete your homework each night (e.g., I do it at home after dinner.)?

Examples of student journal prompts are provided in Figures 3.5 and 3.6.

Figure 3.5 Sample "Advanced" Prompts

1. My favorite activity in mathematics is:

2. The thing(s) I like most about mathematics is (are):

3. What I have liked least about mathematics is:

4. My favorite math teacher was _____ .

   I liked him/her because _____ .

Figure 3.6 Sample "Beginner" Journal Prompts

1. The activity we did this week was _____ .

   I liked/didn't like it because _____ .

2. Three topics that I feel I completely understand are:

   (1)

   (2)

   (3)

   I feel I completely understand these topics for these three reasons:

   (1)

   (2)

   (3)

3. This week I have learned _____

   I still do not understand _____ .

   What I am going to do to help myself learn this is (this may include meeting with a teacher after school) _____ by _____ (date).

4. This week, the topic that we learned about, _____ _____ , is related to the real world (or my life) in this way: _____ . (Explain in detail how this is related to your life, or maybe how it will be in the future; use pictures and examples if it will help you describe your ideas. Use complete sentences.)

Inventories

Teacher and student inventories can also be useful as tools with which to gauge attitude. They allow teachers to learn about students' thinking and beliefs throughout the year. Inventories are different from journals in that students write very little, making them less time-consuming for the teacher to read and the student to complete. A combination of both journals and inventories as shown in Figure 3.7 (NCTM, 1999) may be beneficial to obtain a clearer picture of student attitude toward learning mathematics.

Finally, interviewing a student one-on-one can provide information about how the student feels about learning mathematics. This approach might be more useful for a younger student or one who has difficulties writing. A teacher may ask similar questions to those used for a mathematics autobiography, or any of the journal questions mentioned, as well as any other pertinent questions that can shed light on a student's experience and attitude toward learning mathematics.

For younger students, such as kindergarteners, you might ask them to draw a smiley face, sad face, or question mark to represent their feelings toward mathematics.

HELPING STUDENTS MEET THE CHALLENGES OF REGULAR ROUTINES AND MATERIALS

Homework

Students with learning disabilities face many daily challenges in the classroom. They also face problems when they go home and begin their homework. Many of these students have complex problems that confound them and make independent work very difficult. Often, these students have difficulties remembering what was taught in school that day, they forget to write down assignments, are disorganized, or misplace homework. It is often beneficial for a teacher to give assignments in advance, ensure that they are written in an assignment book, and provide an alternative way for students to get the assignment if they forget what it is, such as a learning buddy they can call or a homework hotline. The following list suggests tips for assigning homework:

- Make sure students can complete the homework as assigned. If not, either suggest a time for extra help or provide a different or modified assignment.
- Whenever possible, allow students time to start the homework assignment in class and check for understanding.

Figure 3.7 Examples of a Mixture of Inventories and Journals

Name _____

Date _____

1. The work I did today:

2. Today I did _____ did not _____ finish my work.

   What I did not finish was:

   I did not finish because:

3. Today I did _____ did not _____ participate in class.

4. Comments about my work:

- State the homework assignment verbally and write it on the chalkboard or overhead projector. Designate a place in the room where students can check for homework assigned.
- Posting assignments on a classroom Web site allows learning-disabled students and parents to access the assignment at home.
- Assign homework in small pieces. For example, if a project is assigned, set a series of due dates for different pieces of the project.
- Set clear homework expectations for students, and make parents aware of these expectations.
- Provide frequent feedback about students' progress on their homework.

Textbook

Many students with learning disabilities also have difficulties with reading comprehension, which can impact their learning of mathematics. Some suggestions for facilitating a student's understanding of what they read in a textbook include strategies for before, during, and after reading.

- Pre-teach vocabulary. If the special student needs extra help with this, a paraprofessional or parent volunteer might be assigned to assist.
- Ask students to write predictions of what they think they will learn from reading the section, page, or chapter. Students may also be asked to state what they want to learn from the section.
- Use analogies and visual images. After a student has read a section of the text, ask her to describe what she read in words and/or pictures. Often students have difficulties articulating mathematical ideas, and it is easier to describe them using analogies and pictures. For example, the concept of "between" is sometimes easier to show with a picture than to describe. Or the concepts of "less than" and "greater than" can be easily demonstrated with objects such as lima beans (one group with 4, another with 6).
- Create concept maps. Concept mapping is the strategy employed to create a special form of a graphic organizer for exploring knowledge and gathering and sharing information. A concept map consists of cells that contain a concept, item, or question and links. The links are labeled and denote direction with an arrow symbol. The labeled links explain the relationship between the cells. The arrow describes the direction of the relationship and reads like a sentence. For an example of a concept map, see Chapter 5.

Be sure to provide instruction for students about the components of their textbook as well as how to use it. Many students do not realize that

(Text continues on page 57)

Table 3.1

Strategy Checklist

Strategy	Information Processing					Language		Cognition and Metacognition	Disposition Toward Learning	Good for All Learners	Can Be Incorporated in Regular Lesson
	Visual	Auditory	Memory	Motor	Attention	Expressive	Receptive				
Mnemonics	X	X	X		X	X	X	X		X	X
Graph paper	X			X						X	X
Extra time on exams/tasks	X	X	X	X	X	X	X	X		X	X
Tape recorder	X	X	X	X	X	X	X	X		X	X
Written and verbal assignments and directions	X	X	X	X	X		X			X	X
Large font	X				X					X	X
Books on tape	X	X	X								
Increase white space on paper	X			X	X	X	X	X		X	X
Preferred seating for students	X	X			X					X	X
Template to isolate sentences or paragraphs in a text	X		X	X	X	X	X				
Use at least 18-point font on overhead	X				X	X				X	X

Table 3.1 (Continued)

Strategy Checklist

| Strategy | Information Processing | | | | Attention | Language | | Cognition and Metacognition | Disposition Toward Learning | Good for All Learners | Can Be Incorporated in Regular Lesson |
	Visual	Auditory	Memory	Motor		Expressive	Receptive				
Photocopy notes from the board or overhead	X	X	X	X	X	X	X			X	X
Colored chalk/overhead pens	X		X		X		X			X	X
Stencil/finger tracing	X			X						X	X
Concrete or pictorial representations	X	X	X		X	X	X	X		X	X
Slow rate of speech		X	X		X		X			X	X
Use appropriate language/vocabulary		X	X				X			X	X
Minimize number of written problems	X			X		X				X	X
Orally assess student	X			X							
Note taker/carbon paper	X	X	X	X		X				X	X
Attention cues	X	X	X		X			X		X	X
Maintain eye contact with students		X		X					X	X	
Structured environment	X		X		X		X	X		X	X

Table 3.1 (Continued)

Strategy Checklist

Strategy	Information Processing					Language		Cognition and Metacognition	Disposition Toward Learning	Good for All Learners	Can Be Incorporated in Regular Lesson
	Visual	Auditory	Memory	Motor	Attention	Expressive	Receptive				
Variety in lessons	X	X	X		X		X	X	X	X	X
"Think aloud"	X	X	X		X			X		X	X
Strategy usage	X	X	X	X	X	X	X	X	X	X	X
Simplify directions and explanations	X	X	X		X		X	X	X	X	X
Analogies	X	X	X	X	X		X	X	X	X	X
Concept maps	X	X	X		X		X	X	X	X	X
Require written and verbal communication	X	X	X		X	X	X	X	X	X	X
Frequent feedback	X	X	X	X	X	X	X	X	X	X	X
Mathematics autobiographies									X	X	X
Inventories									X	X	X
Interviews									X	X	
Journal writing			X			X		X	X	X	X
Color code numbers by place value	X		X		X		X	X		X	X
Clear transitions		X	X	X	X			X		X	X
Parallel assignment			X			X		X		X	X

Table 3.2

Strategy Checklist
(Reproducible)

Student Name _____

Strategy	Information Processing					Language		Cognition and Metacognition	Disposition Toward Learning	Good for All Learners	Can Be Incorporated in Regular Lesson
	Visual	Auditory	Memory	Motor	Attention	Expressive	Receptive				
Mnemonics											
Graph paper											
Extra time on exams/tasks											
Tape recorder											
Written and verbal assignments and directions											
Large font											
Books on tape											
Increase white space on paper											
Preferred seating for students											
Template to isolate sentences or paragraphs in a text											
Use at least 18-point font on overhead											

Table 3.2 (Continued)

Strategy Checklist
(Reproducible)

Student Name _____

Strategy	Information Processing					Language		Cognition and Metacognition	Disposition Toward Learning	Good for All Learners	Can Be Incorporated in Regular Lesson
	Visual	Auditory	Memory	Motor	Attention	Expressive	Receptive				
Photocopy notes from the board or overhead											
Colored chalk/ overhead pens											
Stencil/ finger tracing											
Concrete or pictorial representations											
Slow rate of speech											
Use appropriate language/vocabulary											
Minimize number of written problems											
Orally assess student											
Note taker/carbon paper											
Attention cues											
Maintain eye contact with students											
Structured environment											

(Continued)

55

Table 3.2 (Continued)

Student Name _____

Strategy Checklist
(Reproducible)

Strategy	Information Processing					Language		Cognition and Metacognition	Disposition Toward Learning	Good for All Learners	Can Be Incorporated in Regular Lesson
	Visual	Auditory	Memory	Motor	Attention	Expressive	Receptive				
Variety in lessons											
"Think aloud"											
Strategy usage											
Simplify directions and explanations											
Analogies											
Concept maps											
Require written and verbal communication											
Frequent feedback											
Mathematics autobiographies											
Inventories											
Interviews											
Journal writing											
Color code numbers by place value											
Clear transitions											
Parallel assignment											

important ideas are often set in bold, in color, or in special boxes to set them apart from the text.

CONCLUSION

At first it can seem to be an overwhelming task to teach students with learning disabilities; their difficulties with learning can often appear to be monumental. As a teacher learns about the intricacies of each student and how they approach mathematical tasks, she can adapt instruction to include these individual needs. It is important for all teachers to know their students. The strategies described in this chapter address many of the major problem areas for students with learning difficulties. In Table 3.1, strategies are matrixed to specific challenges a teacher may encounter among her students. A reproducible version in Table 3.2 provides a blank chart, which teachers may use to record what they plan to incorporate in order to promote learning for specific students. The next chapter will discuss a process for assessing your students using an observation checklist of "look fors" in order to plan for instruction.

Assessing 4
Your Special
Education
Students

This chapter will describe a process of observing more closely a student who is having difficulties in mathematics. It does not replace the assessment by a special education teacher or building resource person and the IEP team. However, it offers a structure for paying close attention to how a student learns mathematics. This is intended to help teachers better observe and understand their students' strengths and weaknesses, specifically regarding mathematics. This multidimensional assessment begins with an investigation of the student's readiness for the mathematics content that is planned for the class. The assessment focuses on the student's strengths, which may be used as avenues to teach mathematics to the student, as well as weaknesses, which may impact the student's ability to learn. When completed, this assessment will increase the teacher's knowledge of the student, especially in relation to the content area of mathematics, and facilitate planning to include all student needs in instruction. It is important to note that this assessment technique is not just for students with disabilities. This is an excellent means for a teacher to obtain an understanding of any student's strengths and weaknesses in order to plan for instruction.

This chapter answers the following questions:

- Whom should I assess?
- How can I assess my students' strengths and weaknesses?

- What criteria should I use?
- Why is an assessment important?
- How can this assessment information help me plan for instruction?
- Can I easily assess my student?
- How much time will this take?

Examples of assessments for the students mentioned in Chapter 1, Amanda, Dominick, and Elizabeth, are also included.

WHOM SHOULD I ASSESS?

There are a variety of students whom a teacher may want to assess. The most obvious first choices for assessment are those students who have been referred and are currently receiving special education services, students who are in the process of being referred, and other students who are having obvious difficulties learning mathematics. It may also be useful to complete this assessment for every student in a class. The information that can be obtained regarding how students learn best and what their strengths and weaknesses are will be helpful when teaching any student.

Why should I assess my student? How is this information different from information on the IEP?

This type of assessment will help a teacher understand the student as thoroughly as possible—even students who have IEPs. Although IEPs contain essential information about a student's current level of educational performance in mathematics and the desired outcomes of that plan, these plans are frequently lacking in several critical areas. First, these plans do not often address a wide range of mathematics content areas as suggested by the National Council of Teachers of Mathematics (NCTM, 2000); they focus on basic-skill acquisition. Since IEPs lack breadth regarding topics in mathematics, they often do not include adequate descriptions of what a student can or cannot do in relation to the topics which make up the classroom teacher's planned curriculum. Often, information about how students process and learn information is disregarded, as is their general disposition toward learning mathematics. Finally, IEPs are typically deficit models and do not often address what a student *does* know or *can* do.

This assessment process is designed to help the classroom teacher feel more prepared. Coupled where applicable with the IEP and the help of a special education resource, the teacher will be more ready to recognize and support special needs within her classroom.

How will I assess?

There are two primary tools of this assessment process:

- the asking of probing questions to see more deeply into student thinking
- the "look fors" to guide ongoing observation of students at work

Probing questions, like the examples in Figure 4.1, are used to gain more information regarding how a student thinks and solves problems. They provide an extremely productive means of obtaining more useful information from a student. For students not classified as special education students, the teacher may find that these questions go right to the root of a student's problem and that the answers suggest specific remedies, like remediation of an underlying deficiency.

Alternatively, this process may raise questions that the teacher will want to broach with a special education teacher or other building resource. Without training in special education, it can be very difficult for any educator to accurately assess the cause of the problem a student is exhibiting. However, the informed daily observation by a classroom teacher provides a broader base of information and facilitates more thoughtful and collaborative conversations with the special educator about how to help struggling students. Teachers who use this process can raise their own sensitivity so that student difficulties become more apparent to them. They internalize a deeper understanding of what to look for and a quicker recognition of what they see and how they can help.

Probing Questions

Probing questions are useful to delve more deeply into students' understandings and misconceptions about a concept. Follow-up questions are used subsequent to the probing questions, if enough information is not obtained from the initial question. Figure 4.1 suggests some possible student responses to mathematics activities, possible probing questions that may be used, and follow-up questions.

When will I have time to complete this assessment?

This assessment can be completed in multiple ways and at a variety of times. Assessments may take place within class instructional time. They may also be completed on an individual basis before or after school, at lunch, or during class while other students are pursuing another task. These assessments can typically be completed while observing a student for a few minutes as he performs several different tasks in a regular mathematics class. A teacher may want to complete this whole assessment at the

Figure 4.1 Sample Probing Questions for Student Responses to Activities

Student Response	Probing Question(s)	Follow-up
Student is unable to answer a word problem.	Can you explain to me where you were stopped in answering the question?	Ask the student to read the problem out loud and then ask what the problem is looking for.
Student shows incorrect answer with no work or answers a question incorrectly.	Can you show what you did to get that (answer)? and/or Can you explain to me how you solved that problem?	Provide the student with manipulatives that may be useful to represent and solve the problem. Ask student to show a representation of the question being asked.
Student correctly solves a problem but shows little or no work.	Can you show/explain to me another way to solve this problem?	What operation did you use to solve this problem and why?
Student solves a problem correctly; however, the work shown does not logically lead to the given answer.	Can you show/explain to me why you decided to solve the problem the way you did?	Can you show me how you solved this using a picture, or manipulative?
Student shows correct thought process/work in solving the problem; however, the answer is incorrect.	Is your answer reasonable given the question? What should you do once you have solved a problem?	What are possible estimation strategies you could use to solve this problem? How do you help yourself remember to check your answer?

beginning of the year, working with a student one-on-one. Another option is to complete the assessment based on mathematics topics as they are encountered throughout the year.

What areas should I focus on to gain information about my student?

It is as important to highlight what students know and can do as is it is to identify what they do not know or have difficulty accomplishing. It is based on a student's strengths that a teacher can instruct the student on new information and remedy her weaknesses. The following are very broad areas in which to explore a student's strengths and weaknesses:

- Developmental readiness with respect to a wide range of age-appropriate mathematical topics. Students should be learning concepts and skills that their age-appropriate peers are also learning.
- Information processing (Areas to focus on: visual, auditory, motor, memory, attention)
- Language (expressive and receptive)
- Cognition and metacognition
- Disposition toward learning mathematics

We have looked at how challenges in these areas can impact learning and at strategies to compensate. Here we will create a checklist of observational "look-fors" to assess needs and progress.

Look Fors With Struggling Students

The "look fors" in each of the focus areas in this chapter are certainly not inclusive of all behaviors a teacher may examine when assessing his student. This is a simple structure that can help the teacher obtain some quick but essential information about the student with learning challenges or disabilities. By using the "look fors" in the next section and summarized in the checklist provided in Figure 4.2, a teacher can gain a picture of how individual students are challenged, where they need strategy development, and where strengths can be leveraged.

Developmental Readiness

This component of the assessment process refers to the student's developmental readiness in relation to age-appropriate topics and concepts in mathematics. It is important to include mathematical goals that are linked to the classroom curriculum and to NCTM guidelines (NCTM, 2000), and to assess the developmental milestones appropriate for the concept. For

(Text continues on page 67)

Figure 4.2   Observation Checklist of "Look Fors"

Name:

Area of Difficulty	Yes/No/Not sure	Observations
Information Processing		
Approach		
Does the student prefer to use manipulatives to solve a problem?		
Does the student prefer to use paper and pencil to draw his answer?		
Summary Comments		
Visually		
Does the student lose her place on a page?		
Does the student have difficulty copying numbers?		
Does the student reverse numbers?		
Does the student have difficulty reading multi-digit numbers?		
Does the student have difficulty discriminating between operation symbols?		
Summary Comments		
Auditory		
Does the student have difficulties hearing patterns in counting?		
Does the student have difficulty paying attention in class?		
Does the student have difficulties with decimals?		

(Continued)

Figure 4.2 (Continued)

Name:

Area of Difficulty	Yes/No/Not sure	Observations
Does the student have difficulty with oral drills?		
Does the student have difficulty with dictated assignments?		
Summary Comments		
Motor		
Does the student have difficulty writing?		
Does the student's writing appear to be a normal size?		
Is the writing accurate?		
Summary Comments		
Memory		
Can the student recall information easily (i.e., math facts)?		
Does the student easily retain information taught previously (within the last day, month, and year)?		
Summary Comments		
Attention		
Does the student maintain attention throughout a lesson in a manner that is age appropriate?		
Summary Comments		
Language		

Figure 4.2 (Continued)

Name:

Area of Difficulty	Yes/No/Not sure	Observations
Expressive: Does the student have difficulty explaining how he solved a problem?		
Expressive: Does the student find rapid oral drills difficult?		
Expressive: Does the student have difficulty counting on?		
Summary Comments		
Receptive: Does the student have difficulty with relating vocabulary words to their meaning?		
Receptive: Does the student have difficulty with words that have multiple meanings?		
Receptive: Does the student have difficulty writing words from dictation?		
Receptive: Does the student respond well to verbal/written directions?		
Receptive: Does the student take in information in an age-appropriate manner?		
Summary Comments		
Cognition and Metacognition		
Does the student have difficulties identifying and selecting appropriate problem-solving strategies?		

Figure 4.2 (Continued)

Name:

Area of Difficulty	Yes/No/Not sure	Observations
Does the student have difficulties generalizing, organizing information, and evaluating problems for accuracy?		
Does the studen appropriately monitor her abilit to solve problems?		
Summary Comments		
Disposition toward learning mathematics		
Past experiences learning mathematics: What are the student's earliest memories of mathematics?		
Past experiences learning mathematics: What are the student's favorite areas of mathematics? Favorite teachers?		
Past experiences learning mathematics: What does the student like least about learning mathematics, and why?		
Behaviors: What are the student's behaviors while learning mathematics? Observe the position in which the student sits while completing math.		
Behaviors: Does the student pay attention in math class?		
Attitude toward learning mathematics: How does the student see himself as a learner of mathematics?		
Summary Comments		

example, if a student exhibits a difficulty with a particular concept, a teacher may want to look to previously learned concepts to check for complete understanding. Figure 4.3 provides some examples of mathematics topics along with some areas of conceptual knowledge that a teacher may want to explore if a student is having difficulty learning that concept.

The National Council of Teachers of Mathematics (2000) Standards for grade levels PreK–2, 3–5, 6–8, and 9–12 form the basis on which many schools determine a curriculum for all students. The Standards for grades PreK–2 include these topics: number and operations, algebra, geometry, measurement, data analysis and probability, problem solving, reasoning and proof, communication, connections, and representation. Descriptions of each strand can be found in Chapter 5 or in the *Principles and Standards for School Mathematics* (NCTM, 2000), which are also online at www.nctm.org.

As an example, one aspect of number and operations that a first-grade teacher may want to assess for understanding is that of grouping. A first-grade student should be able to group objects into twos, threes, and fours. Other developmental milestones related to number and operations that are important for students in this age range include one-to-one correspondence and place value, which is fundamental to understanding so many topics in mathematics.

In addition to assessing conceptual understanding in the number strand, teachers also need to assess students' computational fluency. Recent research on the development of mathematical knowledge offers strong evidence that computational fluency and number sense are closely related (Griffin & Case, 1997). Computational fluency involves accuracy, efficiency, generalization, and application of knowledge when solving problems. The concept of numbers and their relationships are the foundation for all mathematics and are necessary for higher learning. NCTM defines computational fluency as the ability to choose and carry out the appropriate method of computation in a given problem. For example, when solving a problem using a calculator, it is essential that students understand the operations used so they can judge whether or not the output is correct.

One specific area of mathematics that many teachers find their students with learning disabilities have difficulty with is learning basic facts. Many learning-disabled students have persistent trouble "memorizing" basic number facts in all four operations (Fleischner, Garnett, & Shepherd, 1982), despite a great deal of effort expended trying to do so. In addition to memorizing basic mathematical concepts (getting them into long-term memory), the most common difficulties occur with efficient *recall* of basic arithmetic facts and reliability in written computation (Gersten & Chard, 1999).

This lack of number sense, basic facts, and computational understanding may impact a student's future understanding of mathematics. There is

Figure 4.3 Math Topics and Conceptual Knowledge

This figure provides some examples of mathematics topics along with some areas of conceptual knowledge that a teacher may want to explore if a student is having difficulty learning a specific concept.

Addition (single- and double-digit)
- Place value
- Grouping
- One-to-one correspondence

Subtraction (single- and double-digit)
- See previous addition-area difficulties
- Composing and decomposing numbers from 1–10, and 11–20

Multiplication (multi-digit)
- Fluency with multiplication facts
- Place value
- Applications of the distributive property

Division (long division)
- Fluency with multiplication facts
- Subtraction
- Place value

Decimals (use of operations with)
- Place value
- Fractions
- Operation difficulties

Fractions
- Equivalency
- Part/Whole
- Place value

Shapes (Geometry)
- Sorting (seeing like/different)
- Generalization
- Set/subset relationships
- Orientation

Data Analysis (Grades 3–5)
- Graphing
- Reading data from a table
- Drawing conclusions from data (predictions)
- Organization skills

a growing belief that many of the difficulties students encounter in pre-algebra and algebra stem from their lack of understanding of whole numbers. In particular, Schifter (1999) has made the case for an emphasis on the development of operation sense as crucial to this preparation for algebra instruction. Thus there is a critical need for students to have a deep understanding of number sense, for teachers to focus on place value, and to be sure students understand the basic operations and their relationship to each other. These are areas that teachers will want to assess and may need to strengthen whenever they see a student struggling.

Here are some suggestions when assessing and observing readiness:

1. *Provide the student with activities that the student would be completing in the regular mathematics classroom curriculum.* Avoid choosing an activity that is significantly different in either content or difficulty level than what the student does in the classroom.

2. *Use probing questions to reveal the specific area of difficulty.* For example, if a student cannot solve a word problem, ask the student what she is having difficulties with when attempting the problem. This will provide more information about what the student understands as well as what she does not understand. Sometimes a student may not know how to answer a question, and the teacher will need to follow with more specific inquires to learn more. A student may have difficulty reading the problem, understanding a vocabulary word, or may not know how to solve the problem. Without asking the student what the specific problem is, a teacher might never identify the difficulty.

Information Processing

Assessing information processing is significant to understanding how a student perceives and stores types of information such as visual and auditory. A description of the information-processing model was previously described in Chapter 2. Briefly, this model is an attempt at describing how sensory input is perceived, transformed, reduced, elaborated, stored, retrieved, and used (Swanson, 1987). Some difficulties related to information processing are memory deficiencies, visual deficits, auditory problems, motor disabilities, memory deficiencies, and attention deficits. Each of these areas should be explored to obtain a clearer picture of a student's strengths and weaknesses when learning mathematics.

As there are many aspects of each of these deficiencies/disabilities, it may be beneficial, when possible, to collaborate with a special education professional to decipher the exact nature of the difficulty. For example, a first-grade student who is having difficulties writing numbers correctly may have motor disabilities; however, there are also other possibilities: The student may have never been taught how to correctly write her numbers, or she may have visual-processing difficulties and reverse her numbers.

Here are some suggestions when assessing and observing this area:

1. *Observe the student while the student is completing a typical activity drawn from the regular mathematics curriculum.* You want to see the student in an environment in which she would normally be working, to see how she approaches problems.

Look for the following:
- *Approach:* Does the student prefer to use manipulatives to solve a problem? Prefer to use paper and pencil to draw the answer?
- *Visual:* Does the student lose her place on a page? Have difficulty copying numbers? Reverse numbers? Difficulty discriminating between operation symbols? Reading multi-digit numbers?
- *Auditory:* Does the students have difficulties hearing patterns in counting? Difficulties paying attention in class, with decimals, oral drills, or with dictated assignments?
- *Motor:* Does the student have difficulty writing? Does the writing appear to be a normal size? Is it accurate?
- *Memory:* Can the student recall information easily (i.e., math facts)? Does the student easily retain information taught previously (within the last day, month, and year)?
- *Attention:* Does the student maintain attention throughout a lesson in a manner that is age-appropriate?

2. *Use probing questions to clarify observations.* For example, if a student has solved a problem incorrectly, a teacher may ask the student to explain how he solved the problem. It is important to clarify the trouble the student is having solving the problem. Does the student understand the question? Does the student know strategies to use to solve the problem, and is he able to utilize a strategy to do so? Does the student have a conceptual understanding of the topic?

When making observations, keep each of the above questions in mind, and when necessary, discuss them with a special educator. For example, if a student has difficulty paying attention in class, it may be that he has an auditory deficit or attention deficit, and more information needs to be obtain before diagnosis and instructional decisions can be made. Observations and anecdotal notes that a teacher makes in these areas will help to make such decisions.

Language Skills

NCTM (1989, 2000) has emphasized the importance of being able to communicate mathematically and explain one's thought process in solving problems. When assessing language skills, it is important to consider a student's ability with directions and explanations, experiences with verbal requirements of word problems, and the student's ability to explain answers. Deciphering the difference between students with expressive problems and those with receptive difficulties impacts the selection of strategies for instruction.

If a student has difficulty explaining how he arrived at an answer, strategies to remedy expressive language difficulties would be implemented, such as using concrete or pictorial models to minimize the verbal formulation. This is a different choice from a strategy used to help students who have difficulties *perceiving* information. For example, a teacher might help students who have difficulty perceiving information by presenting a visual representation of a new concept or vocabulary to tie to the verbal meaning. Assessing a student's language skills can be accomplished by observing while a student is explaining his solution to a problem (among other situations) in front of the class, in a small-group setting, or in a one-on-one situation with the teacher.

Here are some suggestions when assessing and observing this area:

1. *Observe the student while she is completing a typical activity in the regular mathematics class curriculum.*

Look for the following:
- *Expressive:* Does the student have difficulty explaining how she solved a problem? Difficulty counting on? Trouble with rapid oral drills?
- *Receptive:* Does the student have difficulty with relating vocabulary words to their meaning? Or difficulty with words that have multiple meanings? Trouble writing words from dictation? How well does the student respond to directions? Does the student take in information in an age-appropriate manner?

2. *Using probing questions for clarification.* For instance, if a student cannot explain how he solved the problem, would it be easier for the student to demonstrate with a manipulative or draw a picture? Is it that he does not understand the problem, or just cannot explain how to solve the problem? If necessary, these probing questions may be asked in private after a student has completed a problem in the class.

After having assessed these behaviors in the student, the teacher will find it helpful and in some instances necessary to consult a special educator, because various difficulties in these areas could have multiple diagnoses. For example, a student who has difficulties explaining how she completed a problem may either not conceptually understand the problem or may have expressive language difficulties. Likewise, a student who has difficulties with vocabulary may have a receptive language disorder or may have never been exposed to the vocabulary. As stated previously, knowing and understanding your student will provide useful information that can help you successfully include this child in the teaching and learning in your classroom.

Cognition and Metacognition

Cognition refers to understanding. It is the ability to comprehend what is seen and heard, and the ability to infer information from social cues and body language. Metacognition emphasizes self-awareness of how one approaches a task in order to plan and monitor progress. Typically, it is referred to as one's "thinking about thinking." For instance, when a student completes a problem, one example of metacognition would be if the student thinks to himself, "I should check if this answer makes sense and either estimate what the possible answer could be or recheck the answer."

For another example, does the student pick up on social clues in a classroom? How does he respond to directions given in class? Again, the teacher must be careful in interpreting observations without the help of a special educator. It is especially important to assess a student's metacognitive strategies due to the focus in mathematics on problem solving. A teacher might assess this by asking a student to explain her thinking about a problem—specifically what she was thinking, why and how she approached a problem—which may provide some insight into her thinking processes. If a student cannot explain how she completed a problem or why she could not complete it, it might not only be due to metacognitive issues; it could be expressive language problems or a variety of other confounding issues. Consulting with the special educator can help to pinpoint additional strategies. However, all students benefit from using the metacognitive strategies described here. Use some of the following strategies to assess metacognitive or cognitive difficulties:

1. *Observe the student while the student is completing a typical activity in a regular mathematics curriculum and/or in a small-group or one-on-one situation.* Look for the following:
   - *Cognition and metacognition:* Does the student have difficulties identifying and selecting appropriate problem-solving strategies? Does the student have difficulties generalizing, organizing information, and evaluating problems (e.g., determining how best to solve them)? Does the student appropriately monitor his ability to solve problems?

2. *Use probing questions to clarify observations.* For example, ask a student "How do you think you might start this problem?" "What strategies might you use to solve this problem?" You may want to help students along by suggesting they organize the information in the problem or draw a picture to help them understand and solve the problem.

Analyzing a student's issues in this area can be particularly difficult. If a student does not exhibit knowledge of problem-solving processes and how to use them, it may be due to difficulties in cognition or metacognition, or due to lack of exposure to strategy instruction. This area may take longer than the others to observe patterns and determine deficits; however, special education professionals can provide assistance in this critical area.

Disposition Toward Learning Mathematics

A teacher who has taught even one day in a classroom realizes that a positive attitude toward learning is essential for learning to be successful. Investigating a student's disposition toward mathematics requires attention to many aspects of the student's experience learning and doing mathematics, as well as her thoughts about being a mathematics student. If a student does not see herself as someone who can be successful at learning mathematics, she may not put forth the necessary effort to become successful. If a student has had negative experiences while learning mathematics in the past, it is also important to find out about them and to promote as many positive mathematics experiences for that student as possible.

Here are some suggestions when assessing and observing in this area:

1. *Observe the student in class while the student is completing a typical activity in a regular mathematics curriculum or during a private meeting time.* The student may write answers to questions like those in Figures 3.5 and 3.6 if she is old enough. Younger students or students who are not likely to be as communicative in writing can be interviewed using these questions orally.

Look for the following:

- *Past experiences learning mathematics:* What are the student's earliest memories of mathematics? Favorite areas of math? Favorite teachers? What does the student like least about learning mathematics and why? A student as young as a kindergartener may be asked when he first learned about numbers, though kindergarten students have not usually had sufficiently discouraging experiences with number to foster a negative disposition toward learning mathematics.
- *Behaviors:* What are the student's behaviors while learning mathematics? Observe the position in which the student sits while completing math. Does the student pay attention in mathematics class?
- *Attitude toward learning mathematics:* Ask the student how he thinks of himself as a mathematics student? Does the student think he can learn mathematics?

2. *Use probing questions to clarify observations.* For instance, if a student states that they had a bad experience in second grade in mathematics, the teacher may want to clarify the issue further in order to better teach the student. This

could be done either by asking more questions in a one-on-one meeting with the student, or by providing written feedback with questions to the student.

By developing facility with observing students at work and asking probing questions, a teacher will grow in her ability to help her most challenged students.

AMANDA

Amanda is a rather typical sixth-grade student with attention-deficit disorder. Her work lacks organization, and her inability to focus prevents Amanda from comprehending information presented in math class in the same manner or at the same rate as other students. This makes it difficult for her to draw upon that information and subsequently apply it to other problems of similar nature.

The activities used to assess Amanda's understanding of mathematics were selected based on the teacher's knowledge of her and the content to be taught in sixth grade, and some activities were chosen in order to assess her learning skills such as processing. Amanda's teacher observed her difficulties on exams and quizzes and was puzzled, as she often thought Amanda knew more than she was able to express on these assessments. Her teacher was particularly interested in learning about how Amanda approached a variety of problems, so she would know how to best teach Amanda.

(Text continues on page 81)

Figure 4.4   Observation Checklist of "Look Fors" for Amanda

Name: Amanda

Area of Difficulty	Yes/No/Not sure (when applicable)	Observations
Information Processing		
Approach		
Does the student prefer to use manipulatives to solve a problem?	Yes	Amanda prefers to work with objects when solving the fraction, logic, and geometric problems. These are topics that Amanda admits she "does not know as well." It seems as if she prefers concrete models when first learning a topic and once she feels comfortable she no longer needs to rely on them to complete a task.

Name: Amanda

Area of Difficulty	Yes/No/Not sure (when applicable)	Observations
Does the student prefer to use paper and pencil to draw her answer?	Yes	(see notes below)
Summary Comments		Introduce new concepts or topics concretely. For example, when introducing the concept of factor to Amanda, she may need a concrete representation to fully create meaning for herself before she moves into the pictorial or symbolic learning. Amanda may indicate conceptual understanding or mastery of a topic by not choosing to use a concrete manipulative.
Visually		
Does the student lose her place on a page?	Yes	Often, Amanda will lose her place on a page and mix information from separate problems on a page in a book or an exam.
Does the student have difficulty copying numbers?	Yes	She often mixes up information as previously stated.
Does the student reverse numbers?	No	
Does the student have difficulty reading multi-digit numbers?	No	
Does the student have difficulty discriminating between operation symbols?	Yes/No	This can happen when she is copying work from the board or out of a book.
Summary Comments		Amanda may have difficulty with visual processing, as too much information on a

(Continued)

Name: Amanda

Area of Difficulty	Yes/No/Not sure (when applicable)	Observations
		page confuses her and she is then unable to complete an activity correctly. In addition, she may have difficulty copying information from a board or overhead projector and should be provided with copies of the notes. Also, more "white space" around a problem is helpful.
Auditory		
Does the student have difficulties hearing patterns in counting?	No	
Does the student have difficulty paying attention in class?	Yes	Amanda often has difficulties paying attention in class. She is diagnosed as AD/HD.
Does the student have difficulties with decimals?	No	
Does the student have difficulty with oral drills?	No	
Does the student have difficulty with dictated assignments?	No	
Summary Comments		Amanda seems to have strengths in auditory processing. As much as possible, information should be presented verbally as well as in written form. Any assessments should be provided verbally. She seems to remember much more of what is told to her

(Continued)

Name: Amanda

Area of Difficulty	Yes/No/Not sure (when applicable)	Observations
		verbally than visually. In a conversation with her tutor, she mentioned that Amanda seems to know what is required of her when asked verbally; however, when she is asked the same question on an exam, she may not get it correct.
Motor		
Does the student have difficulty writing?	No	
Does the student's writing appear to be a normal size?	Yes	
Is the writing accurate?	Yes	
Summary Comments		No problems observed in this area.
Memory		
Can the student recall information easily (i.e., math facts)?	Yes	Once Amanda has learned information, she will remember it easily.
Does the student easily retain information taught previously (within the last day, month, and year)?	Yes/No	If Amanda has not been engaged in class, she may not remember what is taught.
Summary Comments		Amanda is aware of her difficulties learning mathematics, and as such she creates her own tools to help her learn. Once she has learned something, Amanda will easily utilize this information.

(Continued)

Name: Amanda

Area of Difficulty	Yes/No/Not sure (when applicable)	Observations
Attention		
Does the student maintain attention throughout a lesson in a manner that is age appropriate?	No	Amanda is often not able to pay attention in mathematics class. As previously noted, she is diagnosed with AD/HD. Her inattention is a significant problem that interferes with her ability to obtain information from the teacher in class. This fluctuates depending on when she has last taken her Ritalin.
Summary Comments		Attention issues are crucial for Amanda and her success in mathematics.
Language		
Expressive: Does the student have difficulty explaining how she solved a problem?	No	Amanda does a good job of explaining the problems she solves correctly. She can clearly articulate what she knows and what she does not know about a problem.
Expressive: Does the student find rapid oral drills difficult?	No	
Expressive: Does the student have difficulty counting on?	No	
Summary Comments		Amanda is a very verbal student who usually knows and can explain her mathematical thoughts.
Receptive: Does the student have difficulty with relating vocabulary words to their meaning?	No	Amanda needs new vocabulary pre-taught before usage.
Receptive: Does the student have difficulty with words that have multiple meanings?	No	

(Continued)

Name: Amanda

Area of Difficulty	Yes/No/Not sure (when applicable)	Observations
Receptive: Does the student have difficulty writing words from dictation?	No	
Receptive: Does the student respond well to verbal/written directions?	Yes/Verbal	Amanda follows directions well, and when explanations are given verbally she does very well. She does need directions given both verbally and in writing.
Receptive: Does the student take in information in an age-appropriate manner?	Yes	Amanda seems to have strengths in this area. She benefits from having problems read aloud to her.
Summary Comments		Amanda needs to have directions given to her both verbally and in written form. She may need to have exams and quizzes read to her to be able to fully demonstrate her understanding of a concept. Amanda should be encouraged to verbally rehearse information that she needs to place in long-term memory. This should be communicated to all those who work with Amanda so that they can reinforce this strategy.
Cognition and Metacognition		
Does the student have difficulties identifying and selecting appropriate problem-solving strategies?	No	

(Continued)

Name: Amanda

Area of Difficulty	Yes/No/Not sure (when applicable)	Observations
Does the student have difficulties generalizing, organizing information, and evaluating problems for accuracy?	No	
Does the student appropriately monitor her ability to solve problems?	Yes	
Summary Comments		No problems in this area have been observed.
Disposition toward learning mathematics		
Past experiences learning mathematics: What are the student's earliest memories of mathematics?		Amanda states that she has mostly failed throughout her experiences learning mathematics. Her earliest memories are of confusion in first grade.
Past experiences learning mathematics: What are the student's favorite areas of mathematics? Favorite teachers?		She does comment on one time in her life when she felt confident in mathematics, third grade. However, her success is attributed to her "great" third-grade teacher. When she does do well in class, she believes that it is just "good luck" and not her own ability to do mathematics.
Past experiences learning mathematics: What does the student like least about learning mathematics, and why?		Amanda doesn't like very much about mathematics. She says it is just hard.
Behaviors: What are the student's behaviors while learning mathematics? Observe the position in which the student sits while completing math.		Amanda will often draw in mathematics class, though she says she is paying attention when she is drawing.

(Continued)

Name: Amanda

Area of Difficulty	Yes/No/Not sure (when applicable)	Observations
Behaviors: Does the student pay attention in mathematics class?		Amanda often has difficulty paying attention in mathematics class; however, she is only disruptive to herself. Once she is reminded to pay attention, she will remain on task.
Attitude toward learning mathematics: How does the student see herself as a learner of mathematics?		Amanda is frequently commenting that she is "just not good at mathematics," that she "cannot do mathematics," she "does not have a mathematical brain like her dad and her sister."
Summary Comments		Amanda's lack of self confidence about learning is a serious problem for her. Each time Amanda is successful with a new concept or skill, the process by which she approaches this should be identified so that she begins to take responsibility for her successes.

DOMINICK

Dominick, a second-grade student, is somewhat typical of a mildly learning-disabled student who is experiencing problems across the board in both language and math. His strengths include a willingness to try, cooperation, as well as the ability to handle basic computation.

The activities used to assess Dominick were chosen based on the content to be taught in second grade and in order to evaluate information processing, and preferred mode of instruction. Dominick's teacher had observed in class the difficulty he had expressing himself and completing word problems. As a result, word problems were chosen to evaluate his problem-solving skills, and other problems were selected to assess his understandings of specific mathematics content such as geometry and number sense.

(Text continues on page 87)

Figure 4.5 Observation Checklist of "Look Fors" for Dominick

Name: Dominick

Area of Difficulty	Yes/No/Not sure (when applicable)	Observations
Information Processing		
Approach		
Does the student prefer to use manipulatives to solve a problem?	Yes	Dominick appears to prefer using concrete models to represent what he understands.
Does the student prefer to use paper and pencil to draw his answer?	Yes	If manipulatives are not available, Dominick will draw pictures.
Summary Comments		Dominick has difficulty expressing himself and can frequently explain his answers using concrete or pictorial models.
Visually		
Does the student lose his place on a page?	Yes	Dominick does lose his place often when reading.
Does the student have difficulty copying numbers?	No	
Does the student reverse numbers?	No	
Does the student have difficulty reading multi-digit numbers?	No	
Does the student have difficulty discriminating between operation symbols?	Yes	He often confuses signs such as addition and subtraction.
Summary Comments		Dominick seems to enjoy activities which are visually presented; new information should be presented in this manner whenever possible.
Auditory		
Does the student have difficulties hearing patterns in counting?	Not sure	I am unsure if Dominick does not understand what is being said

(Continued)

Name: Dominick

Area of Difficulty	Yes/No/Not sure (when applicable)	Observations
		to him in terms of his language or if he has difficulty processing what I am saying.*
Does the student have difficulty paying attention in class?	Yes	Dominick often appears to be "fooling around" in class.
Does the student have difficulties with decimals?		Not relevant for a student in his age range.
Does the student have difficulty with oral drills?	No	See previous answer*
Does the student have difficulty with dictated assignments?	No	See previous answer*. At times, Dominick seems to understand when I speak with him one-on-one. This is dependent on the task though.
Summary Comments		An area of great concern for me. I am unsure if Dominick is having difficulty following directions because of language issues or auditory processing issues.
Motor		
Does the student have difficulty writing?	No	
Does the student's writing appear to be a normal size?	Yes	
Is the writing accurate?	Yes	
Summary Comments		No problems noted in this area.
Memory		
Can the student recall information easily (i.e., math facts)?	No	Dominick has difficulty retrieving mathematics facts above six plus six when asked spontaneously.
Does the student easily retain information taught previously (within the last day, month, and year)?	No	Dominick has difficulty learning new information and this can often interfere with his ability to retain new information.

(Continued)

Name: Dominick

Area of Difficulty	Yes/No/Not sure (when applicable)	Observations
Summary Comments		Dominick needs more familiarity with the basic facts in order to insure quick retrieval from his long-term memory. Dominick should be given the opportunity to use manipulatives whenever needed. He should also be taught strategies to facilitate information transferring from his short-term memory to long-term memory such as mnemonics.
Attention		
Does the student maintain attention throughout a lesson in a manner that is age appropriate?	No	At times he seems as if he is distracted in class; this may also be due to an inability to understand the language.
Summary Comments		I am not sure if Dominick has difficulty paying attention, or if it is due to cognitive or first-language difficulties.
Language		
Expressive: Does the student have difficulty explaining how he solved a problem?	Yes	Dominick often has difficulty explaining his reasoning verbally in class. When he is asked to show how he completed a task, he is usually able to do so; however, sometimes he loses his train of thought and needs support from his peers or the teacher.
Expressive: Does the student find rapid oral drills difficult?	Yes	

(Continued)

Name:

Area of Difficulty	Yes/No/Not sure (when applicable)	Observations
Expressive: Does the student have difficulty counting on?	Yes/No	He has difficulty counting on with larger numbers.
Summary Comments		Dominick appears to have difficulty expressing himself verbally. It is not clear if he has a focusing deficit which interferes with his attending in class or if he cannot interpret directions due to visual-processing problems or weak language background.
Receptive: Does the student have difficulty with relating vocabulary words to their meaning?	Not sure	Dominick has difficulty expressing his thoughts, and at times it is difficult to determine if he has difficulty with vocabulary.
Receptive: Does the student have difficulty with words that have multiple meanings?	Not sure	(see above box)
Receptive: Does the student have difficulty writing words from dictation?	No	When Dominick is paying attention, he is able to write words from dictation.
Receptive: Does the student respond well to verbal/written directions?	No	When Dominick is given directions verbally or in written form, he often does not seem to understand what is asked of him or does not appear to be paying attention. When given directions individually, Dominick can often complete assignments successfully.
Receptive: Does the student take in information in an age-appropriate manner?	No	

(Continued)

Name:

Area of Difficulty	Yes/No/Not sure (when applicable)	Observations
Summary Comments		More information needs to be gathered form the special-education teacher to determine if Dominick has attention-deficit difficulties, visual-processing or language-barrier problems, or a combination. Until more information can be gathered about his language deficits, directions should be given individually and new information should be given both verbally and visually. Vocabulary should also be explicitly taught and tied to a concrete representation.
Cognition and Metacognition		
Does the student have difficulties identifying and selecting appropriate problem-solving strategies?	Yes/No	He has difficulty when he does not understand the task.
Does the student have difficulties generalizing, organizing information, and evaluating problems for accuracy?	No	Once Dominick gets started on a problem, he can usually follow through successfully.
Does the student appropriately monitor his ability to solve problems?	Yes	
Summary Comments		Dominick appears to not have difficulty solving problems if he understands the problem.
Disposition toward learning mathematics		
Past experiences learning mathematics: What are the		Dominick seems to enjoy mathematics

(Continued)

Name:

Area of Difficulty	Yes/No/Not sure (when applicable)	Observations
student's earliest memories of mathematics?		and says he liked math last year.
Past experiences learning mathematics: What are the student's favorite areas of mathematics? Favorite teachers?		None
Past experiences learning mathematics: What does the student like least about learning mathematics, and why?		He says he likes working with blocks and drawing.
Behaviors: What are the student's behaviors while learning mathematics? Observe the position in which the student sits while completing math.		Dominick sits appropriately in a group setting.
Behaviors: Does the student pay attention in mathematics class?		At times, Dominick appears to be unengaged in learning mathematics.
Attitude toward learning mathematics: How does the student see himself as a learner of mathematics?		Dominick says he loves math class.
Summary Comments		Dominick does not seem to have developed a dislike for mathematics. In fact, he likes math class and says it is one of his favorite times of the day in school. Lack of positive attitude does not seem to be an issue for Dominck.

ELIZABETH

Elizabeth is a quiet fourth-grade student. She turns in homework most days, but many problems are incorrect or incomplete. Elizabeth can recite her mathematics facts and uses them for math computation efficiently. Her weaknesses are primarily focused on solving word problems. When she begins the process of problem solving, she tends to have difficulty analyzing the question and developing a plan to solve the problem. She has relatively good success with solving a word problem once she has guided support with setting it up.

(Text continues on page 94)

Figure 4.6   Observation Checklist of "Look Fors" for Elizabeth

Name: Elizabeth

Area of Difficulty	Yes/No/Not sure (when applicable)	Observations
Information Processing		
Approach		
Does the student prefer to use manipulatives to solve a problem?	Yes	Elizabeth will reach for manipulatives to solve problems she is either not completely familiar with solving or that are new to her.
Does the student prefer to use paper and pencil to draw her answer?	Yes	If Elizabeth is comfortable with a topic, she will often draw the problem out on paper.
Summary Comments		Elizabeth enjoys "seeing" the mathematics (using manipulatives or drawings) and is much stronger at learning new concepts when they are presented in this manner.
Visually		
Does the student lose her place on a page?	No	
Does the student have difficulty copying numbers?	No	
Does the student reverse numbers?	No	
Does the student have difficulty reading multi-digit numbers?	No	
Does the student have difficulty discriminating between operation symbols?	No	
Summary Comments		Elizabeth does not seem to have difficulties copying, reversing numbers, reading multi-digit numbers, or deciphering operation symbols.

(Continued)

Name: Elizabeth

Area of Difficulty	Yes/No/Not sure (when applicable)	Observations
Auditory		
Does the student have difficulties hearing patterns in counting?	No	
Does the student have difficulty paying attention in class?	No	
Does the student have difficulties with decimals?	No	
Does the student have difficulty with oral drills?	No	
Does the student have difficulty with dictated assignments?	No	
Summary Comments		No problems in this area were observed.
Motor		
Does the student have difficulty writing?	No	
Does the student's writing appear to be a normal size?	Yes	
Is the writing accurate?	Yes	
Summary Comments		No problems in this area were observed
Memory		
Can the student recall information easily (i.e., math facts)?	Yes	
Does the student easily retain information taught previously (within the last day, month, and year)?	No	Elizabeth seems to have trouble in this area when learning a new concept that requires more than one step.

(Continued)

Name: Elizabeth

Area of Difficulty	Yes/No/Not sure (when applicable)	Observations
Summary Comments		Elizabeth seems to have appropriate long-term retrieval skills evidenced by her accurate recall of math facts. However, she seems to have difficulty working to assimilating multiple pieces of information together. For example, she has difficulty with multi-step word problems. Does this indicate difficulties with her short-term memory? One area that appears to need help is getting information from Elizabeth's short-term memory into long-term memory. Once the information is in her long-term memory, she seems able to recall information adequately. Strategy instruction should be provided to facilitate her learning.
Attention		
Does the student maintain attention throughout a lesson in a manner that is age appropriate?	Not sure	
Summary Comments		At times, Elizabeth seems to drift off; this is usually when she does not appear to understand a topic. At other times, it appears age appropriate.
Language		
Expressive: Does the student have difficulty explaining how she solved a problem?	No	

(Continued)

Name: Elizabeth

Area of Difficulty	Yes/No/Not sure (when applicable)	Observations
Expressive: Does the student find rapid oral drills difficult?	No	
Expressive: Does the student have difficulty counting on?	No	
Summary Comments		Elizabeth has no difficulty articulating her logical reasoning when she clearly understands a topic. At times, she seems to get lost (when solving word problems); however, she can express that she has lost her way when that occurs.
Receptive: Does the student have difficulty with relating vocabulary words to their meaning?	No	Once a vocabulary word has been appropriately introduced, Elizabeth easily understands it.
Receptive: Does the student have difficulty with words that have multiple meanings?	No	
Receptive: Does the student have difficulty writing words from dictation?	No	
Receptive: Does the student respond well to verbal/written directions?	Yes	Elizabeth can easily understand directions; however, it may appear she does not if she does not understand how to complete the work.
Receptive: Does the student take in information in an age appropriate manner?	Not sure	Elizabeth learns new information easily except for multi-step problem solving.

(Continued)

Name: Elizabeth

Area of Difficulty	Yes/No/Not sure (when applicable)	Observations
Summary Comments		Elizabeth seems to take in information well and responds appropriately to written and verbal directions.
Cognition and Metacognition		
Does the student have difficulties identifying and selecting appropriate problem solving strategies?	Yes	She has difficulty solving multi-step problems.
Does the student have difficulties generalizing, organizing information, and evaluating problems for accuracy?		Elizabeth has difficulties with solving word problems. Often, she cannot explain how she would solve a word problem. When she does get started she seems to lose her place quickly. She also has difficulty estimating an appropriate answer and explaining what strategies to use when solving a problem.
Does the student appropriately monitor their ability to solve problems?	Yes/No	Elizabeth is aware she had difficulties solving word problems. However, she does not seem to have any strategies to monitor this problem.
Summary Comments		Elizabeth needs help with strategies to help her solve multi-step problems. She says she is often "lost" when it comes to solving word problems.
Disposition toward learning mathematics		
Past experiences learning mathematics: What are the student's earliest memories of mathematics?		Helping her mom fold socks. She used to have to count them for her mother.

(Continued)

Name: Elizabeth

Area of Difficulty	Yes/No/Not sure (when applicable)	Observations
Past experiences learning mathematics: What are the student's favorite areas of mathematics?; Favorite teacher(s)?		Elizabeth says she enjoyed mathematics when she was in Kindergarten and first grade when she used to use lots of manipulatives. Her first grade teacher has been her favorite teacher because she always let her use manipulatives in class. She does not like when teachers do not let her use manipulatives or draw her answer out.
Past experiences learning mathematics: What does the student like least about learning mathematics, and why?		She admits she understands basic computation, however, also admits to difficulties problem solving.
Behaviors: What are the student's behaviors while learning mathematics? Observe the student's position in which they sit while completing math.		As soon as Elizabeth feels she cannot do a problem she tends to give up and will either draw, daydream or do something non-mathematically related.[*]
Behaviors: Does the student pay attention in mathematics class?		Usually (see above)[*]
Attitude toward learning mathematics: How does the student see themselves as a learner of mathematics?		Elizabeth is a very shy student who does not feel as if she is a particularly strong student in mathematics.
Summary Comments		It appears that Elizabeth has experienced a great deal of failure when problem solving. She engages easily in topics she feels comfortably with and understands.

CONCLUSION

With practice, the regular teacher can become an insightful observer and skillful questioner to identify students' strengths, understandings and misunderstandings, and gaps in necessary underlying skills and knowledge. Thus armed, the teacher can better help all students learn. Once again, observations will be most productive when considered along with the information from the IEP and consultation with a special education resource.

By comparing observations that emerge from the checklist of look fors in Figure 4.2, along with ongoing observations and assessments, a teacher can look back at the strategy matrix in Chapter 3 (Figure 3.7), and can put into place strategies to accommodate the challenged learners in the classroom. Chapter 5 will position the challenged students within the larger context of the standards-referenced mathematics classroom, and discuss more general strategies for teaching special and low-achieving learners. In most instances, these approaches and modes of instruction will also benefit the entire class.

General Strategies for Teaching Inclusive Mathematics to All Students 5

This chapter will position the instructional inclusion of special and challenged learners in the larger context of mathematical standards and best teaching practices for all students. The ways in which these strategies presented here can be particularly effective in promoting understanding among the learning-disabled students in your classroom are noted.

STANDARDS FOR ALL

Investigations into the teaching of mathematics support the theory that "less is more." Focusing on fewer key concepts leads to greater overall student achievement over time. Compared to other countries that significantly outperform the United States on tests, our schools do not challenge students to learn important topics in depth (National Center for Education Statistics [NCES], 1996). American schools tend to include many more ideas in an average lesson, and develop fewer of them in depth (Stigler & Hiebert, 1999). Research has shown that a curriculum that focuses on learning fewer concepts in-depth is beneficial (Clements, 2000), and a rigorous curriculum is crucial for all students especially those with learning disabilities (Maccini & Gagnon, 2002). Further, Rivera, Taylor, & Bryant, (1994/1995) state that all students, including those with disabilities, should be taught concepts identified in the *Principles and Standards for School Mathematics* (NCTM, 2000).

In an attempt to strengthen reform-based mathematics, the National Council of Teachers of Mathematics (NCTM) published the 2000 *Principles and Standards for School Mathematics.* This document presents six principles and ten standards as a framework for a high-quality mathematics education. The six principles NCTM puts forth as comprising the foundation of all mathematics education are:

- *Equity.* This principle supports the view that there should be high expectations and strong support for all students.
- *Curriculum.* The curriculum principle refers to having a cohesive curriculum that focuses on important mathematics, clearly articulated across the grades.
- *Teaching.* Effective teaching requires an understanding of what students know, what they need to know, and then challenging and supporting them to learn it well.
- *Learning.* Students must build on their prior experiences and knowledge, and actively learn mathematics with understanding.
- *Assessment.* Assessment should support learning of meaningful mathematics and be informative for both the student and the teacher.
- *Technology.* Essential to teaching and learning of mathematics is the utilization of technology. It influences what the students are taught and enhances their learning (NCTM, 2000, pp. 11–27).

The Standards are guided by five main goals, which envision that students

- become better problem solvers,
- learn to reason mathematically,
- learn to value mathematics,
- become more confident in their mathematical ability, and
- learn to communicate mathematically (NCTM, 1989, 2000)

The Standards include five mathematical content strands describing the content students should learn: number and operations, algebra, geometry, measurement, and data analysis and probability. Lastly, five mathematical processes highlight the ways of acquiring and using the content knowledge: problem solving, reasoning and proof, communication, connections, and representation. In essence, the focus of the Standards is to improve conceptual understanding rather than teaching procedural knowledge.

Instructional programs from kindergarten through Grade Twelve should include each of these content and processing strands, enabling all students to understand and apply mathematics effectively.

- Number and Operations
  - understand numbers, ways of representing numbers, relationships among numbers, and number systems;
  - understand meanings of operations and how they relate to one another;
  - compute fluently and make reasonable estimates.
- Algebra
  - understand patterns, relations, and functions;
  - represent and analyze mathematical situations and structures using algebraic symbols;
  - use mathematical models to represent and understand quantitative relationships;
  - analyze change in various contexts.
- Geometry
  - analyze characteristics and properties of two and three-dimensional geometric shapes and develop mathematical arguments about geometric relationships;
  - specify locations and describe spatial relationships using coordinate geometry and other representational systems;
  - apply transformations and use symmetry to analyze mathematical situations;
  - use visualization, spatial reasoning, and geometric modeling to solve problems.
- Measurement
  - understand measurable attributes of objects and the units, systems, and processes of measurement;
  - apply appropriate techniques, tools, and formulas to determine measurements.
- Data Analysis and Probability
  - formulate questions that can be addressed with data and collect, organize, and display relevant data to answer them;
  - select and use appropriate statistical methods to analyze data;
  - develop and evaluate inferences and predictions that are based on data;
  - understand and apply basic concepts of probability.

Paralleling these content areas are the process standards:

- Problem Solving
  - build new mathematical knowledge through problem solving;
  - solve problems that arise in mathematics and in other contexts;
  - apply and adapt a variety of appropriate strategies to solve problems;
  - monitor and reflect on the process of mathematical problem solving.
- Reasoning and Proof
  - recognize reasoning and proof as fundamental aspects of mathematics;
  - make and investigate mathematical conjectures;
  - develop and evaluate mathematical arguments and proofs;
  - select and use various types of reasoning and methods of proof.
- Communication
  - organize and consolidate mathematical thinking through communication;
  - communicate their mathematical thinking coherently and clearly to peers, teachers, and others;
  - analyze and evaluate the mathematical thinking and strategies of others;
  - use the language of mathematics to express mathematical ideas precisely.
- Connections
  - recognize and use connections among mathematical ideas;
  - understand how mathematical ideas interconnect and build on one another to produce a coherent whole;
  - recognize and apply mathematics in contexts outside of mathematics.
- Representation
  - create and use representations to organize, record, and communicate mathematical ideas;
  - select, apply, and translate among mathematical representations to solve problems;
  - use representations to model and interpret physical, social, and mathematical phenomena.

An underlying assumption of the mathematics reform movement is that the mathematics pedagogy and curricula is effective for all students, including low achievers. However, the *Principles and Standards* set forth by NCTM (2000) offer few, if any, guidelines for how the Standards might be modified for students who are at risk of academic failure or have a learning disability in mathematics. Baxter, Woodward, & Olson (2001) discovered that low-achieving students are only minimally involved in standards-linked, reform-based mathematics lessons. Low achievers are often marginal members of a community of learners and typically remain silent or distracted during whole-group discussions. Group discussions, which are an ongoing interplay of cognitive and metacognitive processes used in successful problem solving, can tax the low-achieving students' listening and thinking skills. Low-achieving students typically lack the prerequisite skills and usually need more time to review concepts from previous years. By being aware of these issues, teachers can make changes and modifications as they deem appropriate, and can try to leverage available time, building expertise, resources, paraprofessional and other support personnel, peer tutors, and volunteers to provide special and discouraged learners with the critical supports that they need for success.

TEACHING MATHEMATICS FOR UNDERSTANDING

According to Mercer & Mercer (1998), three steps are important for teaching the acquisition of both computation and problem-solving skills: assessment of a student's prior knowledge of mathematics, obtaining a commitment from the student to learn mathematics, and using effective teaching skills to teach mathematics.

At the time of introduction of new concepts and skills, it is important to consider whether a student has the necessary prerequisite skills (Bley & Thornton, 1995; Stein, Silbert, & Carnine, 1997; Witzel, Smith, & Brownell, 2001). This information can be gathered through detailed observation and probing questions as described in Chapter 4, which offer a means to know each individual learner.

Goal setting with the student is also extremely beneficial. Mercer and Mercer (1998) have found that both elementary and secondary students with learning problems respond well to goal setting in mathematics. Goal setting enables the students to be proactive in their own education. Studies confirm that students perform better when they have helped determine their own goals, rather than having them set for them. Some suggestions for goal setting with students include the following: arrange a consistent time (e.g., daily, weekly) when you meet with a student to discuss her current performance, future learning goals, and how they will be measured.

This discussion should also focus on students taking responsibility for their own learning. For example, if a student fails a task, and has not either attempted the task or put effort into it, it should be pointed out to the student that his effort was directly related to his failure. Conversely, students who have used appropriate strategies or put effort into a task and been successful should be made aware that their success is based on their efforts and not luck. This approach helps give the students "ownership" for their learning progress and a sense of personal control, rather than letting them attribute both success and setback purely to luck and other external factors.

PROBLEM SOLVING IN MEANINGFUL CONTEXTS

The mathematics that students learn should be taught within a meaningful problem-solving context. According to the theory of situational cognition, students gain deeper understandings of curriculum when they actively construct knowledge in contexts that they find meaningful and motivating (Greeno, 1993; Greeno & The Middle School Mathematics Through Applications Project Group, 1998). Student understandings develop and are associated with the circumstances in which they were learned, which implies that teachers should structure learning experiences using contexts that students will recognize in new situations. This is an important aspect of transferring learning, which is a major difficulty for students with special needs. Further, embedding the problem-solving information within a real-world context helps students activate their conceptual knowledge when presented with a real-life problem-solving situation (Gagne, Yerkovich, & Yerkovich, 1993) and improves student motivation, participation, and generalization (Polloway & Patton, 2001).

Traditionally, mathematics has been viewed as a set of rules that require memorization, with the tacit assumption that computational problems are always solved using algorithms, and that problems always have one correct solution. Problem solving was formerly portrayed as students solving word problems. NCTM in its *Principles and Standards for School Mathematics* (2000), states, "A major goal of mathematics programs is to create autonomous learners, and learning with understanding supports this goal. Students learn more and learn better when they take control of acquiring knowledge by defining their goals and monitoring their progress. When challenged with appropriately chosen tasks, students become confident in their ability to tackle difficult problems, eager to figure things out on their own, flexible in exploring mathematical ideas and trying alternative paths, and willing to persevere (p. 21).

Word Problems and Problem Solving: Related and Distinct

What does problem solving mean? Polya (1962) defined problem solving as searching for an appropriate course of action to attain an aim that is not immediately attainable. This definition can apply not only to traditional "word problems," but also to the more open-ended and "messy" unstructured problems that fall within the current understanding of "problem solving." Both kinds of problems promote development of valuable thinking and problem-solving skills.

Students should be provided with the opportunity to solve problems in a variety of contents; good problems often integrate multiple topics and involve significant mathematics. According to NCTM (2000), students should be able to build new mathematical knowledge through problem solving. As students solve meaningful problems, they should solidify the mathematics they already know, extend their knowledge to include more mathematics, and develop fluency with skills. Students should be encouraged to solve problems that arise in mathematics and in other contexts. For example, students may be curious about which type of cereal has more raisins. They should be encouraged to apply and adapt a variety of appropriate strategies to solve the problem, and in the process, the concept of probability may arise and be discussed. In addition, students should be provided with the opportunity to monitor and reflect on the process of mathematical problem solving.

Much of the research regarding problem solving and students with learning disabilities focuses on word problems. Difficulties with problem solving are not unique to students with disabilities. Bryant, Bryant, and Hammill (2000) state that word-problem solving remains a challenging task for all students that demands instructional attention in schools. However, traditionally, problem solving has been a particularly troublesome area for students with special learning needs (Thornton & Jones, 1996). These students have a hard time with metacognitive and cognitive processing, which makes it difficult or impossible for them to choose appropriate strategies, reflect on their usage (Brownell, Mellard, & Deshler, 1993; Mercer, 1997), and then transfer this knowledge from one area to another. In order to problem solve, a student needs to

- have a mathematical knowledge base,
- be able to apply acquired knowledge to new and unfamiliar situations, and
- actively engage in thinking processes

These thinking processes involve having a student

- recognize a problem,
- plan a procedural strategy,
- examine the mathematical relationships in the problem, and
- determine the mathematical knowledge needed to solve the problem.

Further, the student needs to

- represent the problem,
- generate an equation,
- estimate an answer,
- sequence the steps,
- compute the answer, and
- check it for reasonableness (Mercer & Mercer, 1998).

This is a tall order. Problem solving is a complex task for even the strongest of students. Thus, along with teaching skills and concepts explicitly, strategy instruction and problem solving, include teaching students to recognize and use the above task breakdown, should also be taught explicitly. Patten, Cronin, Bassett, and Koppel (1997) recommend teaching students with learning problems to be proficient problem solvers in dealing with everyday situations and work settings. The following is a typical problem-solving sequence: "Read the problem carefully," "analyze or identify important aspects of the problem," "draw or write the problem," "solve the problem," and "check the answer" (Miller, Butler, & Lee, 1998).

Significantly, Xin and Jitendra (1999) found that instruction in solving word problems improved the performance of students with learning difficulties and promoted the maintenance and generalization of the skill. A number of guidelines for problem-solving instruction follow, some of which reflect overall recommended practice with challenged learners:

- Link instruction to students' prior knowledge and help them connect the new knowledge to previously learned information. For example, when introducing the concept of division (new knowledge), a connection relating multiplication (prior knowledge) to division (division is the inverse of multiplication), and demonstrating that division (new knowledge) is repeated subtraction (prior knowledge) are useful links to facilitate learning of the new concept. When solving new problems (new knowledge), a teacher may want to link prior knowledge (previously learned strategies such as making a table to organize information) to help build a student's repertoire of problem-solving strategies.
- Teach students to understand operations and concepts rather than procedures. If two-digit multiplication is taught procedurally, it will often be memorized and not be meaningfully learned. However, if students first see that multiplication is really repeated addition, they will learn more deeply and meaningfully.
- Use problems that students can relate to and that pertain to daily life. This promotes meaningful learning.

- Teach word problems simultaneously with computational skills.
- Facilitate development of a positive attitude toward mathematics.
- Teach students learning strategies, such as metacognitive strategies, that help them become independent learners.

The following sections will describe instructional strategies that research has found to facilitate students' learning of mathematics within a problem-solving curriculum.

CONSTRUCTIVIST TEACHING OF MATHEMATICS

NCTM supports a constructivist approach for teaching mathematics. This instructional approach assumes that students are naturally active learners who construct new personalized knowledge via linking prior knowledge and new knowledge. Students are taught within an authentic context (problem-solving activities that enable students to attach meaning and relevance to the learning task), and they make connections between classroom activities and real-word problem solving (Cobb, Yackel, & Wood, 1992). During this time, the teacher and the students participate in a collaborative dialogue, and the teacher facilitates instruction within each students zone of proximal development (range of learning where a student is appropriately challenged but not overwhelmed) (Vygotsky, 1978). Constructivist learning places substantial demands on the learner and poses significant difficulties for the student with learning disabilities. These students may need teacher and peer support to help them compensate for difficulties with the following components of constructivism (Mercer, Jordan, & Miller, 1996):

- Having sufficient prior knowledge to construct new and appropriate meaning; understanding connections between prior learning and new information. Students with learning disabilities often have severe learning discrepancies in mathematics (Mastropieri, Scruggs, & Shiah, 1991).
- Attending to teacher presentations, and interactions between teacher and students and student and student. Often students with learning disabilities have difficulties maintaining attention (Garnett, 1992; Zentall & Ferkis, 1993).
- Using cognitive and metacognitive processing to acquire, remember, and construct new mathematical knowledge. Students with learning disabilities often have deficiencies in both of these areas (Brownell, Mellard, & Deshler, 1993).

- Being active participants in their own learning. Many students with learning disabilities have histories of failure in mathematics. These often contribute to a low self-esteem and negative outlook on their mathematical abilities (Maccini & Gagnon, 2000).
- Engaging in group discussions to solve math problems. Students with learning difficulties can exhibit a range of difficulties with regard to language skills both receptive and expressive (Bley & Thornton, 1995). In addition, lack of social skills can be problematic for these students (Bos & Vaughn, 1994).
- Becoming self-regulated learners. Self-regulated learners are aware of their own learning characteristics, develop their own metacognitive characteristics, and maintain a proactive attitude about learning. Students with learning disabilities have been described as passive learners, and typically do not actively participate in or self-regulate their learning.

This does not mean that students with disabilities cannot be taught in a constructivist manner. Using a constructivist continuum for instruction allows for education of a diversity of learners. This suggests movement along a continuum either toward explicit instruction or the opposite direction toward implicit as student learning needs require. Students who have learning difficulties need more explicit help in becoming self-regulated, proactive learners. Where explicit instruction is needed, it should be provided.

EFFECTIVE INSTRUCTION

Research has found several instructional components to be effective in math instruction of students with learning disabilities, as well as other learners. The teacher should provide

- An advanced organizer. The teacher should connect new information to previously learned skills, state the new topic to be learned, and provide a rationale of why this new information will be learned.
- Modeling. The teacher should model strategies for problem solving
- Guided practice. Students should be allowed time to practice the new skill with teacher guidance.
- Independent practice. After guided practice, students should practice the new skill independent of the teacher's help.
- Feedback.
- Generalization. (Adapted from Maccini & Hughes, 2000, and Mercer & Miller, 1992, as cited in Gagnon & Maccini, 2001)

Direct Instruction

Teacher-directed instruction is a primary component for teaching mathematics to students with learning disabilities (Borkowski, 1992; Bryant, Bryant & Hammill, 2000; Wilson & Sindelar, 1991). Cobb, Yackel, and Wood (1992) also emphasize the necessity for direct instruction in helping students learn mathematical concepts and relationships. Direct instruction is instruction in which the teacher serves as the provider of knowledge. This is based on the premise that when learning is complex and difficult for learners, the teacher must provide extensive support to facilitate student understanding. The teacher offers an explanation or model of a skill or concept, guides the student through the application in a variety of concepts, and provides multiple opportunities for independent practice toward successful mastery and generalization. Direct instruction emphasizes student mastery. Students are explicitly taught concepts, procedures and strategies, and new vocabulary (Bryant, Bryant, & Hammill, 2000).

Direct instruction includes the following components (Maccini & Gagnon, 2000):

- explicit modeling of strategy use
- feedback (error corrections)
- mastery learning
- generalization
- cumulative reviews of previously learned information

Modeling of Strategies

Modeling has been found to be an important component for teaching cognitive skills such as verbal mathematics problem solving (Bos & Vaughn, 1994; Witzel, Smith, & Brownell, 2001). In this process, the students are watching the teacher model the appropriate behavior as well as listening to her self-talk or thinking aloud. One strength of modeling is that students can experience both the observable and unobservable behaviors (self-talk). As previously noted, it is important that teachers not only model mathematical algorithms, but that they explicitly model cognitive and metacognitive strategies in solving word problems (Hutchinson, 1993a; Montague, 1993). Further, researchers have found that specific strategy instruction in mathematics holds significant promise for students with learning problems.

Explicitly teaching both cognitive and metacognitive strategies has been found to be effective when teaching students with learning disabilities (Montague, Applegate, & Marquard, 1993; Hutchinson, 1993a; Cassel & Reid, 1996). In these studies, despite differently worded strategy steps, similar processes emerge for solving word problems.

Typically, students were cued to

"read the problem carefully,"

"analyze or identify important aspects of the problem,"

"draw or write the problem,"

"solve the problem," and

"check the answer."

In each of these studies, students were systematically instructed using teacher demonstrations, modeling, and feedback for the strategy and provided time to appropriately learn the strategy (Miller, Butler, & Lee, 1998). An example of a second-grade teacher modeling by thinking aloud how to solve a mathematics problem appears below.

Modeling a "Think Aloud"

Teacher: "First I am going to read the problem aloud to the class. I have seven nickels, three dimes, and four quarters. If I want to buy a large candy bar that costs $ 1.05 with tax, how much money will I have left?

"OK. Class, I am going to show you how I would go about solving a problem like this. I am going to say aloud all of the things that I think to myself as I problem solve. First step I need to take to solve this problem is to read it. (The teacher reads the problem aloud to the class.) Hmm, I think that I first need to know what the problem is asking. The problem says: How much money will I have left after I have bought the candy bar. Now I need to know how much money I have in order to see if I have enough money to buy the candy bar. I am going to add all of the money I have together. I have seven nickels, which is 35 cents, so I will write that down (as she draws the coins with the amount written underneath the coins). Three dimes are 30 cents, and four quarters are equal to $1.00.

"If I add that all up (teacher models on the board or overhead how to add all the numbers together, making sure that the ones, tens, and hundreds are in the correct columns and that the dollar sign and the decimal point are properly cited), I get $1.65. I know that the problem tells me the candy bar costs $1.05, so I need to take that amount from the $1.65 I have in my pocket. (This process is also modeled on the board.) I have 60 cents left after I buy my candy bar. I should also check my answer. I'll add 60 cents to $1.00 (teacher demonstrates how to check the answer by adding the cost of the candy to the amount of money left). I have $1.65, so my answer is correct."

The teacher modeled one method of solving this problem and included her "self talk." As previously mentioned, instruction on multiple strategies should be explicitly taught using direct instruction.

Another example of explicitly teaching strategies is using the mnemonic DRAW. This strategy can be explicitly modeled by the teacher (Mercer, Jordan, & Miller, 1996) and can be useful for students when solving math problems involving computational tasks.

Discover the sign.

Read the problem.

Answer or draw a conceptual representation of the problem using lines and tallies, and check.

Write the answer and check.

STAR is another first-letter mnemonic that is effective for general problem solving (Maccini & Hughes, 2000).

Search the word problem (read the problem carefully, write down facts).

Translate the words into an equation in picture form (e.g., choose a variable, identify the operation, and represent the problem through manipulatives or picture form).

Answer the problem.

Review the solution (e.g., reread the problem, check for reasonableness of the answer).

Mastery Learning and Generalization

As a teacher monitors the progress of a student with disabilities, it is important to teach for mastery learning and generalization. Mastery learning refers to teaching a skill to a level of automaticity. Some benefits of mastery learning are improved retention and ability to solve higher-level problems. Generalization refers to the transfer of learning to another situation. The ability to generalize includes both the ability to deduce the general from the particular case to form a concept and the ability to subsume a particular case under a known concept or generalization (Rachlin, 1998). Many students can successfully complete a task in one setting but not in another. For example, a student may be able to accurately add decimals in mathematics class. However, in science, the same individual may not appear to understand the concept at all. To promote generalization, a teacher should provide opportunities to practice a skill using a wide range of materials at different times and in different situations (Bos & Vaughn, 1994; Mercer & Mercer, 1998).

Generalization is very difficult for students with learning problems (Smith & Luckasson, 1992); it does not appear to occur naturally with these students and must be taught systematically. A teacher may provide prompts or questions to promote generalization to other problem-solving situations, content areas, and real-world situations (Gagnon & Maccini, 2001). Cumulative reviews of material are also necessary to continuously strengthen the ties between new and previously learned information.

Feedback

As students are learning, it is important to continuously monitor their progress and provide positive and corrective feedback. (Gagnon & Maccini, 2001) suggest providing feedback in the following manner: Document student performance (e.g., calculate student performance); target any error patterns/incorrect answers; reteach if necessary; provide student practice with similar problems and monitor student performance; and close with positive feedback. Guided practice should be completed before independent practice is attempted.

Specific information about why a student did not complete a task correctly is important to convey to students with learning disabilities. For example, if a student incorrectly completes a problem in which she was required to add fractions, she needs to be told exactly where there was an error, not just that the problem was incorrect. If a student incorrectly computed the least common multiple, he should be provided with that information and if necessary, re-teaching about the concept. A teacher needs to analyze the errors and provide corrective feedback immediately so that the student does not continue to repeat the same errors. As students become more proficient with a skill or concept, less support will be needed in order for the students to become self-sufficient learners.

Cumulative Reviews

Students with learning disabilities often have difficulties with recalling information previously learned. Cumulatively reviewing previously learned information can help to strengthen ties between new and previously learned information as well as to solidify this knowledge.

VARYING INSTRUCTIONAL GROUP SIZE

In addition to the use of an authentic problem-solving curriculum and the employment of effective instruction principles, there are other effective strategies that can prove useful in working with students with learning disabilities. Varying group size for instruction is one of those strategies (Lock, 1996). Peer tutoring can also be an effective strategy to facilitate instruction (Fasko, 1994; Harper, Mallette, Maheady, Bentley, & Moore, 1995) when teaching counting-on procedures, rote memorization, oral and written drills, and practice using flashcards (Miller, Butler, & Lee, 1998). For older children in elementary grades, dyadic work groups have been found to promote superior mathematics learning compared to traditional, adult-directed instruction for low-, mid-, and high-achieving students as well as those with learning disabilities (Fuchs et al., 1997). Recent research (Fuchs, Fuchs, & Karnes, 2001) has found that using dyads is also effective with students as young as five or six years old, with and without disabilities.

Cooperative groupings are another effective way to teach students with learning disabilities (Rivera, 1996; Johnson & Johnson, 1986); however, some researchers caution that cooperative learning should be integrated with direct instruction (Rivera, Gillam, Goodwin, & Smith, 1996; Slavin, Madden, & Leavy, 1984). Cooperative learning is a desirable instructional strategy because it tends to reduce peer competition and isolation and to promote academic achievement and positive interrelationships. This strategy must be used in a classroom that is supportive of student differences, where the climate is conducive to all students learning. Students must feel that if they fail, they will not be ridiculed by their peers or the teacher. The following sections describe cooperative learning and provide an example of using this strategy with direct instruction.

Cooperative Learning

NCTM (2000) promotes active learning and teaching as well as classroom discourse; cooperative learning is the technique to accomplish these goals. Cooperative learning consists of three major components: lesson preparation, instruction, and evaluation (Rivera, 1996). During the lesson preparation, teachers

- select the mathematics and collaborative objectives to target for instruction and cooperative-learning groups
- plan the math activity
- identify ways to promote the elements of cooperative learning
- identify roles
- establish groups

Content area objectives should come from a variety of sources: curriculum guides, textbooks, the *Principles and Standards for School*

Mathematics (NCTM, 2000), and students' Individualized Education Plans (IEPs). In addition, teachers can use assessment information obtained from probing questions and observations to assess readiness in terms of prerequisite skills and concepts.

According to Johnson and Johnson (1986), there are five basic elements of cooperative learning: positive interdependence, face-to-face interaction, individual accountability, group behaviors, and group processing. Positive interdependence means that students see the importance of working as a team and realize that they are responsible for contributing to the group's effort. Face-to-face interaction involves students working in an environment that promotes working together and discussing mathematics. Individual accountability suggests that students are responsible to the group for completing work. Group behaviors refer to those interpersonal, social, and collaborative skills needed to work with others successfully. Finally, group processing is an opportunity team members have to evaluate both the individuals' and the group's contributions to the collaborative effort.

These important components of cooperative learning can be facilitated in a variety of ways, including the following: assigning students to be responsible for certain tasks (record keeper, leader, checker); providing limited materials, which necessitates sharing; assigning bonus points for demonstrating collaborative behaviors; asking students to self-evaluate after completing a task; assigning a group grade to the math activity; and arranging the activity so that students can interact in small groups.

Lesson instruction refers to the time in which cooperative learning activities occur. Students should engage in cooperative learning activities after they have received direct instruction in the mathematics and collaborative skills or problem-solving activities targeted for the group activity. Providing direct instruction is important so as to reduce the failure of students, particularly those with LD, and to achieve a successful group outcome. Cooperative learning may be used in a variety of ways—as a guided practice time when students engage in tasks to practice newly skills, at the beginning of math instruction as a way of reviewing skills and concepts, to practice a new topic within the context of previously taught material, or for problem solving. As an example, if the math objective is to teach students how to solve word problems using a specific strategy, then the strategy steps should first be taught directly. Students could then engage in a cooperative learning activity that requires the use of the strategy to solve the problems.

To facilitate instruction, the teacher must provide for smooth transitions between the direct group instruction and the cooperative learning activity. This necessitates having all materials and the activity ready ahead of time. The teacher needs to continuously monitor student progress in the small groups and reinforce the frequencies of collaborative behaviors.

In the final component, lesson evaluation, the teacher evaluates the groups' progress in achieving their mathematics objectives and their ability to work collaboratively. For the latter, the teacher may want to explain in advance the rubric that will be used to evaluate their collaboration. The teacher may then encourage students to engage in group and self-evaluations (Rivera, 1996), perhaps again using a rubric such as the one in Figure 5.1. The advance sharing of criteria can help all students to self-regulate. This assessment should be followed up by requiring students to complete individualized assignments based on what they learned from the cooperative activities.

The makeup of the groups can vary; however, only one student with learning disabilities should be placed in a single group. Student roles should be previously assigned, though students should be told to rotate periodically so that all students gain experience in all roles. If possible, bonus points may be distributed occasionally based on each group's demonstration of encouraging and supportive behavior.

Students should be assessed on their understanding at intervals throughout the process. The teacher will informally assess them when they verbally present their work and while they are working in groups. Finally, they will be assessed using a criterion-referenced written examination.

Students will need to review their roles and responsibilities and ask for explanations of how students can encourage and support one another. Clear directions for transitioning into cooperative learning groups should be given. The teacher facilitates learning by helping students with questions and providing further instruction if necessary. Appropriate group behaviors should be reinforced. Time for group processing should follow the activity, at which time the students who are the representatives are called upon to explain the solutions to their problems.

Evaluating the Lesson

Evaluating the students' mastery of the objectives is critical. Several types of assessments may be utilized, and should be based on their appropriateness, such as anecdotal and observational assessments during the group activity, assessments such as posttests following the activity, and a self-evaluation. Students may evaluate themselves with a rubric such as the one in Figure 5.1 that includes self-evaluation regarding their group participation and collaborative skills as well as an evaluation of their content learning.

Coupled with direct instruction, cooperative learning can be an effective instructional strategy that provides students with LD opportunities to practice math skills and concepts, reason and problem solve with peers, use mathematical language to discuss concepts, and make connections to other skills and disciplines.

Figure 5.1   Student Self-Evaluation Rubric for Cooperative Learning

Name: _____

This tool uses a 4-point scale with 1 being the lowest and 4 being the highest.

1. Did I contribute appropriately to the group project?   1   2   3   4

2. Did I work collaboratively?   1   2   3   4

3. What I learned in this project:

4. Things I still do not understand:

This tool may be used as a self-evaluation tool or adapted and used to evaluate a peer or group.

MULTIPLE REPRESENTATIONS

"The ways in which mathematical ideas are represented is fundamental to how people can understand and use those ideas" (NCTM 2000, p. 67). Using multiple representations means selecting one concept and representing it in different ways. For example, when teaching a new concept, a teacher may use words, a diagram, a picture, an equation, a graph, or a symbolical representation. Students with learning difficulties often need multiple methods of viewing a concept in order to understand the concept or skill. They should learn conventional ways of representing their understandings of mathematics to facilitate their learning and their ease in communicating these understandings to others. As students develop their understanding of mathematics, their repertoire of representations increases and becomes more varied. For example, while students in grades K–2 may use concrete representations like blocks, pieces of macaroni or other pasta, sea shells, and pictures to represent mathematics, students in grades 3–5 may model mathematics using tables, graphs, and words. When a student is having difficulty with a concept, revisiting the concrete level may help facilitate his understanding.

One sequence of instruction that research has found to be successful for teaching students with disabilities is the Concrete-Semiconcrete(also known as pictorial)-Abstract sequence (CSA). The CSA sequence is a method of making instruction relevant and using explicit instruction to provide students with hands-on experiences. Hands-on experiences allow students to understand how numerical symbols and abstract equations are operating at a concrete level, making the information more accessible to all students (Maccini & Gagnon, 2000). Teaching students using the CSA sequence enables them to understand the concepts of math prior to memorizing facts, algorithms, and operations. Students who have difficulty in mathematics may need additional resources to support and consolidate the underlying concepts and skills being learned. They benefit from multiple experiences with models and reiteration of the linkage of models with abstract, numerical manipulations. Research has found that using the CSA sequence is an excellent way to teach students with learning problems to understand mathematical concepts, operations, and applications (Harris, Miller, & Mercer, 1995; Mercer & Miller, 1992; Witzel, Smith, & Brownell, 2001).

The CSA sequence requires that students first learn a concept, operation, or application in a concrete manner. For example, at the concrete level when first introduced to the addition of fractions, students may work with the representation of each fraction using pattern blocks, Cuisenaire rods, or Unifix cubes, and represent their answers using these manipulatives. Where these are not available, teachers can substitute inexpensive manipulatives like pennies, pasta, or cereal. For distinguishing between ones and tens, teachers can use two types of pasta. At the semiconcrete or pictorial level, students use two-dimensional drawings (pictures or lines and tallies) to solve computational problems. For example, students may draw a picture of "1/2" with paper and pencil. After successfully solving problems at this level, students move to the abstract level, in which they try to solve problems without using either concrete representations or drawings of the problem. Students will work with solving abstract equations such as 1/4 + 1/5 = __ without the use of manipulatives. Those who have difficulty in mathematics need extensive experience at both the concrete and semiconcrete levels before they can use numerals meaningfully. Since all students will be required to solve problems at the abstract level, achieving mastery is essential (Mercer, Jordan, & Miller, 1996). An example of the CSA approach is found in the example below.

Example of CSA approach:

One day in November, the temperature in Northville, NY, dropped an average of 2 degrees F per hour. If the total temperature change was 10 degrees, how many hours did it take for the temperature to change?

I. Concrete Application

Students can use chips that have black on one side and white on the other to represent positive and negative integers.

Black chip = +1   White chip = −1

Step1: Students begin with no chips; they then count the sets of chips (−2) to get −10.

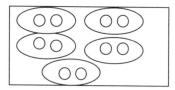

Step 2: Students add 5 sets.

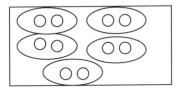

Step3: Students count the number of sets needed (5)

II. Semiconcrete or Pictorial Application

Students draw pictures of the representations.

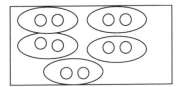

III. Abstract application

1. Students wrote the numerical representation:

−10 ÷ − 2 = # of hours

They solve the expression (either using division, repeated subtraction, or missing addend) and obtain 5 hours. Then re-read and check their answer.

Students also need multiple concrete representations of concepts and of ratios, for example, the meaning of a fraction. A student who is exposed only to equal parts of a circle may come to believe that all equal parts are pie-shaped. Students should be given opportunities to use multiple concrete representations of a fraction, including both discrete and continuous models, in order to learn and generalize the concept of a fraction. They may describe in their own words what "equal parts" means to them, or draw pictures of equal parts.

An example using multiple representations to teach the concept of pattern involves first using manipulatives to concretely represent the pattern, then words to describe the pattern, then numbers to symbolically represent the pattern. The concrete representation of a pattern using blocks such as those with smiley faces and hearts is below.

Students could either write or verbally state the pattern: three smiley faces, one heart, and three smiley faces one heart. Or they might say "face, face, face, heart, face, face, face, heart." And finally, this pattern could be represented using sounds like hand claps and foot stamps, or numbers, 3,1,3,1. Letters may also be used, such as a a a b a a a b.

PROMOTING CONNECTIONS IN MATHEMATICS

The NCTM Standards documents (1989, 1991, 1995, 2000) emphasize making and assessing connections. Hiebert and Carpenter (1992) state that the degree of a student's understanding is determined by the number, accuracy, and strength of connections. Students with learning difficulties often have trouble making connections themselves and need support in making them (Bley & Thornton, 1995; Clements, 2000). For example, it is useful for students to understand the inverse relationship between multiplication and division, as multiplication facts can be helpful when solving division problems. A useful tool to facilitate the student's development of such connections is a concept map. A concept map visually illustrates mathematical connections and describes them in writing.

Concept maps can illustrate hierarchical relationships among ideas, or can take on the form of spider maps, which are used to illustrate webbed relationships, or chain maps, used to illustrate sequential relationships. Concept maps can be an invaluable tool for fostering the meaningful learning of mathematics by students at any level. They are useful when introducing new concepts and connecting them to one another and to known concepts. As previously noted, students with learning disabilities have trouble making connections. Concept maps both help them to do this and help the teacher to see where concept understandings are tenuous, mistaken, or nonexistent. Having students develop their own concept maps also encourages active construction of concepts, fosters metacognitive knowledge and autonomy, motivates conjecture making and testing, and promotes logical reasoning and problem solving (Baroody & Bartels, 2000).

PROMOTING COMMUNICATION

Students with language difficulties need to demonstrate their knowledge of mathematics with concrete materials and explain what they are doing at all ages and all levels of mathematics work, not just in the earliest grades (Herbert, 1985). Etheredge (2000) states that "mathematical discourse that develops a language for talking about problems and their solutions fosters reflection about problem solving and promotes better problem strategies."

Figure 5.2   Concept Maps. The following concept map (hierarchical) is an example of how a sixth-grade student might understand the concept of polygons. The rational numbers concept map is an example of a chain or sequential concept map also drawn by a sixth-grade student. And the shapes map is an example of a spider map completed by a first-grade student.

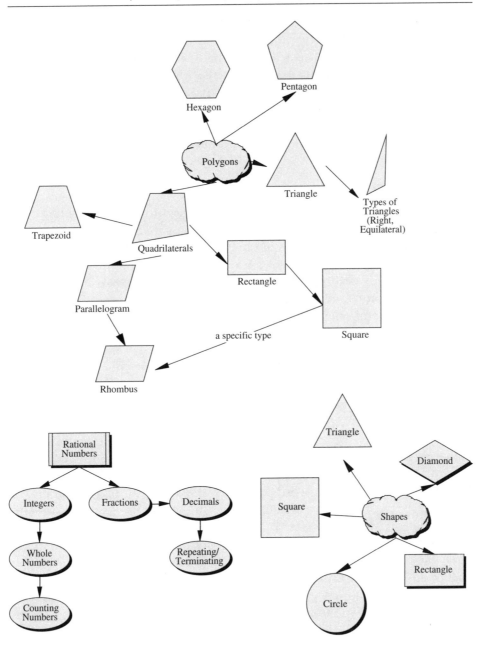

Understanding for all children tends to be more complete when they are required to explain, elaborate, or defend their position to others. The burden of having to explain often acts as the extra push needed to connect and integrate their knowledge in crucial ways (Brown & Campione, 1990).

In particular, many LD students have a tendency to avoid verbalizing in math activities. Developing their habits of verbalizing math examples and procedures can greatly help in removing obstacles to success in general mathematics settings. Advocates of writing in the disciplines believe it is a tool that helps students think better (Sierpinska, 1998; Pugalee, 1997), as they produce, apply, and extend knowledge to make sense for themselves in the same way that mathematicians and scientists do (Connolly, 1989). Various writing approaches can be used to promote the types of thinking and reasoning required in problem-solving situations. The following are some examples of how writing can be used to develop problem-solving methods:

- Writing problems and solutions
- Designing investigations or describing how to solve a problem
- Comparing and contrasting alternative approaches
- Describing how to use technology in solving a problem

The process of writing, which includes planning, composing, and evaluating through recursive actions, is related to the processes involved in reasoning problems in mathematics (Pugalee, DiBiase, & Wood, 1999).

Writing Math Stories/Problems to Promote Student Understanding

One approach to promoting discourse in the mathematics classroom is the Structure-Plus-Writing approach (Rudnitsky, Etheredge, Freeman, & Gilbert, 1995). This approach is designed to help students develop flexible strategies for building representations across a wide variety of arithmetic word problems. Students develop an understanding of problem structure through writing their own word problems based on their own experiences. The teacher begins with a discussion about what the students already know with questions such as, What is a math story? or What is a math story problem? The teacher presents the definition of a math story—any story, happening, or event that has to do with quantities or amounts. The teacher and students discuss the definition and then present examples of different types of stories.

A "something happens story" is one in which something happens to an original or initial quantity; it is increased or decreased. Here is an example of a "something happens problem": Evonne had fourteen candies. Then her brother David ate two of them. How many candies did Evonne have after David ate two candies?

An "altogether story" is a problem in which quantities are put together to form a total amount. For example, Arifa had 21 M&M's, her cousin Albert had 32. How many M&M's did they have together?

A "compare story" is one in which quantities are compared in terms of more, less or fewer, such as, Janice had 11 tennis balls, her friend Becky had nine. How many more tennis balls does Janice have than her friend Becky?

In pairs, the students create their own stories, discuss and categorize the type of story they have created, and are encouraged to write a story of another type than what they have already written. Once students are familiar with the nature of a math story, and understand that there are many questions that can be generated from one math story, the teacher gives examples of math stories and requires the students to write problems to go with them. Students then solve each other's problems, writing comments to the student authors about the challenging or easy nature of each problem they solved. The comments are then reviewed and discussed by the original authors. After students are comfortable with the write/solve/discuss schematic approach, the teacher should develop similar instructional sequences to solve problems with extraneous information and problems where multi-step procedures are required. This instructional process should be adapted to meet the needs of students in a particular classroom.

More ways to promote communication in the classroom include the following:

- Use cooperative grouping. Cooperative learning can be used to promote classroom discourse and oral language development (Rivera, 1996).
- Require students to explain their answers in writing.
- Require students to explain their answers verbally.
- Include journal work as a daily part of mathematics instruction. Students should be encouraged to write about their attitudes and feelings toward learning mathematics, about mathematical ideas, as well as more advanced mathematical concepts.

Communication is integral to helping students develop their mathematical understandings.

PROMOTING A POSITIVE ATTITUDE TOWARD MATHEMATICS

Many students with difficulties learning mathematics develop negative attitudes toward learning mathematics and their capabilities of learning the subject. Poor academic self-concept, low self-esteem, or negative attitudes on the part of students with learning disabilities may be associated with their poor academic and social outcomes (Montague, 1997). Affective variables can impact a student's learning of mathematics; therefore, strategies for fostering a positive attitude toward mathematics should be used in instruction. The following list is a compilation of instructional techniques for addressing affective issues (Licht, 1993; Mercer and Mercer, 1998; Montague, 1997; Montague, Applegate, & Marquard, 1993; Vispoel & Austin, 1995; Sliva & Roddick, 2001):

- Involve students in setting their own goals. These goals should be challenging yet attainable. Monitor this progress on a pre-determined schedule (daily, weekly, etc.), using a graph or some other visual display to show gains in strategy knowledge and usage, effort expended, accuracy, or other variables that may provide a measure of success.
- Ensure success by completing a task analysis for any skill or concept taught. Students should be provided with feedback on each step of the process.
- Make learning meaningful. Provide problems that are relevant to a student's life.
- Communicate clear expectations of success.
- Teach students to attribute their failures to lack of effort or ineffective use of strategies. Explain to students that their own efforts influence their successes and failures.
- Model enthusiasm toward learning and doing mathematics.
- Have students write about their attitudes and feelings toward mathematics.
- Teach students to reinforce themselves for setting goals, using strategies, solving problems, and other effortful tasks.
- Provide the opportunity for students to demonstrate what they have learned for other students, and teach them to compliment one another for trying hard and being successful.
- Structure the classroom around task-oriented goals that emphasize learning mastery. Provide positive reinforcement to students for setting and achieving personal learning goals. Stress how the student is performing relative to the student's past performance.
- Reinforce students for effort on mathematics work, and stress the important role that errors play in learning opportunities.
- De-emphasize goals that foster competition among students. Avoid giving social comparison information and normatively based grades and feedback.

Since students differ in their motivation, self-perception, and attitudes, strategies for increasing positive attitude toward learning mathematics will vary depending on the student. An important component in maintaining a positive attitude toward learning mathematics is to create a classroom environment that is conducive for all learners to learn. Students must feel that if they fail, they will not be punished or ridiculed by the teacher or other peers. A discussion in the first few days of school about the type of behaviors that are acceptable in the class should also include specifics about how students will treat each other. Mistakes should be treated as avenues to success.

Assessment and Feedback

The importance of monitoring a student's progress and providing appropriate feedback cannot be overstated. Gersten, Carnine, and Woodward (1987) have found that teachers who provide immediate corrective feedback produce higher student achievement. It is essential that students be told what components of the process they have completed incorrectly. For example, if a student is asked to compare the fractions 1/2, 1/3, and 1/4, placing the largest fraction first, and they write 1/4, 1/3, 1/2, it is important to ask the student why the 1/4 was written first, and then, based on their answer, to provide corrective feedback as opposed to marking the problem incorrect. If there is no feedback, the student is left to interpret what they think they may have done wrong. With a classroom full of students, it can become difficult to provide immediate corrective feedback to each student. Engaging students in checking their own work, and using peers to help provide feedback, can thereby promote student learning (Bos & Vaughn, 1994).

Traditional standardized testing has been problematic for students with learning disabilities. The recent trend in mathematics education assessment is to select procedures that (a) reflect the curriculum being taught, (b) permit use of materials (e.g., manipulatives, calculators) that are available during instruction, and (c) to include different formats (e.g., pencil/paper, verbal, manipulative) for responding. Assessment procedures may include traditional standardized tests, group problem-solving discussions, and visual displays of manipulatives to depict solutions to problems (Rivera, Taylor, & Bryant, 1994/1995).

Two types of assessments are needed to gain insights into a student's mathematical thinking so as to plan instruction and monitor progress: product assessment and process assessment. Product assessment is used to compare students to their peers, and to determine whether a student has mastered the designated math content. Process assessments (observation, questioning) focus on the problem-solving strategies or procedures used by students. NCTM (1989) calls for the use of multiple assessments to plan and evaluate student learning. Several specific types of assessments include standardized tests, criterion-referenced tests (CRTs), curriculum-based measurement (CBM), non-referenced assessment techniques, and portfolio assessments. These can all provide useful information about an instructional program and the student's understanding of content (Rivera et al., 1994/1995).

Using a variety of assessments is useful for evaluating students with disabilities. It is important to have a range of both product and process assessments in order to have a complete picture of a student's understanding of mathematics.

TECHNOLOGY IN THE MATHEMATICS CLASSROOM

The infusion of technologies such as computers and calculators into schools has required teachers to investigate the new technologies, learn how to use them, and then determine how they may be most appropriately used to facilitate learning. NCTM (2000) says the effective use of technology should

- Allow students to extend their range of accessible computational problems and provide them with more examples or representational forms than are feasible by hand, thus enabling students to execute routine procedures quickly and accurately and freeing more time for making and exploring conjectures, conceptualizing, and modeling;
- Engage and encourage students' ownership of abstract mathematical ideas;
- Offer teachers options for adapting instruction to special student needs;
- Provide unique learning activities in such areas as graphing, visualizing, computing, and access to the Internet and the World Wide Web;
- Provide students access to powerful mathematical ideas at all grade levels by managing complex calculations, organizing and displaying large data sets, graphing functional relationships, producing models and simulations, and creating interactive graphical and geometric environments. (NCTM 2000, pp. 24–27)

NCTM emphasizes that calculators and computers are "essential tools for teaching, learning and doing mathematics. . . . They can support investigation by students in every area of mathematics, including geometry, statistics, algebra, measurement, and number. When technical tools are available, students can focus on decision making, reflections, reasoning and problem solving" (NCTM 2000, p. 24).

Research has focused on many different technologies in the pursuit of facilitating student learning of mathematics using technology. These tools range from hand-held calculators to computers using videodiscs and digital cameras. Recent research has focused on calculators as tools to replace excessive computational practice (Woodward, Baxter, & Robinson (1999), videodiscs for complex mathematical problem solving (Bottge & Hasselbring, 1993), and microcomputers for thematic learning (Zorfass & Copel, 1995). This section will discuss the two most commonly used technologies in the classroom, calculators and computers.

Calculators

For many students with learning difficulties, aspects of computation interfere with their ability to successfully problem solve. These students spend so much time on successfully completing computation that they do not get to the important aspects of problem solving such as concept development and practical application (Bos & Vaughn, 1994). Use of calculators allows students to focus on problem solving rather than on computations; thus, their implementation may be especially helpful for students who have difficulty in this area (Fleischner, Nuzum, & Marzola, 1987). Heddens and Speer (1988) found that calculators can help students develop an understanding of place value, reversibility, relationships among number operations, and mathematical estimates. Further research completed by Hembree and Dessart (1992) suggest the following:

- Calculator use for instruction and testing enhances learning and the performance of arithmetic concepts and skills, problem solving, and attitudes of students.
- Usage of calculators in the early grades is frequently for familiarization, for checking work, and problem solving.
- Attitudes of children using calculators are favorable; unfortunately, some students still feel that using a calculator is similar to cheating.

The following activities can be completed with a nonscientific, algebra logic calculator with pairs of students. These activities are designed to promote mathematical reasoning (Wheately & Clements, 1992).

Guess My Number. This activity can be completed using a variety of methods. Here is an example of one method:

Annie chooses 34 as a mystery number and enters the sequence $34 \div 34 =$ into her calculator. The display shows 1. She hands the calculator to her partner, Steve, and asks, "Can you find my number? (Steve knows division is the operation.) You should enter your guess in the calculator and push the equal key. When the display shows 1, you have found my number."

Steve enters several numbers into the calculator starting with 60; the display shows .56666. He then enters 50 and the display shows .68.

Eventually, Steve notices the pattern and finds the mystery number. Successive experiences completing this activity would deepen Steve's concept of decimals.

The Range Game. This game has been found to promote an understanding of numerical relationships, estimations skills, decimals, and the idea of limits. This activity can be used at any grade level and in a variety of ways. Here is one example:

Students are placed in pairs and asked to find a number that when multiplied by 25 gives another number between 125 and 325. Students are asked to enter 25 in their calculators and choose a number that will give them a number in the range when multiplied by the 25. They are then encouraged to find all whole numbers that will be appropriate. Students should also be challenged to find the smallest and largest numbers that may satisfy the conditions. As students complete this activity, they have an opportunity to construct meaning for decimals and develop number sense.

Calculators can be very useful in the mathematics classroom for students with learning problems. To ensure that students utilize them to the best of their ability, a teacher should give students the chance to first become familiar with their calculators or one provided in the classroom. Students should be instructed in the proper usage of calculators, including how and why they are to be used in their classroom. Finally, all calculators should be stored in working order in a designated area of the classroom.

Computers

Computers have multiple potential uses for students with disabilities. They allow students with motor difficulties to type legible work instead of handwriting it. Many software packages have been developed to facilitate learning for students with disabilities, such as software to translate students' verbal responses to a written format, help students make connections within a content area, develop spatial sense, learn new concepts, and problem solve in real-world situations. A few very useful applications for teaching mathematics are discussed below.

Logo. This application created by Terrapin Software allows students to create geometric figures by typing commands that direct the movement of a "turtle" on the computer screen. As students instruct the turtle to turn right 90, and go forward 10, the turtle leaves a path that it has followed. Research has found that appropriately designed Logo activities can encourage students to think about geometric objects in terms of their components and geometric properties. This promotes higher levels of geometric thought (Clements & Battista, 1989).

Inspiration. Inspiration is a software program that enables a student to create an outline in a traditional format using roman numerals, numbers, and letters, and have it instantly transformed into a Web-like format and vice versa. As previously mentioned, students with learning disabilities have difficulties making connections in mathematics and need support in making them (Bley & Thornton, 1995; Clements, 2000). This tool can be very useful when trying to visually demonstrate connections between concepts in mathematics by developing a concept map. Concept maps may also, of course, be "low-tech," that is, created without technology, using paper and pencil.

World Wide Web/Databases/Microsoft®Excel/Word processing. One very inexpensive way to engage a student in problem solving is by using applications that generally come with any computer. Obtaining real-life information (data) from the World Wide Web has become an engaging way to facilitate meaningful learning through problem solving. Students can gather real-life data from a variety of sources all over the world, use databases to organize and sort the information, analyze the date using Microsoft®Excel, and then write and defend their answers using a word processor.

Computer manipulatives. These have recently become available for student usage. Clements and McMillen (1996) found that computer manipulatives can provide representation as meaningful to students as traditional physical objects. These computer representations may even be more manageable, flexible, and extensible than their physical counterparts.

Research has found that students who use appropriate technology persist longer, enjoy learning more, and make gains in mathematical performance (Babbitt & Miller, 1997). Thus, it is important to carefully select appropriate software for use in the classroom. Some sound considerations for software selection in the mathematics classroom are stated below. Software should be chosen that has the following attributes (Babbitt, 1999):

- a simple screen display—the simpler the better
- modifiable attributes
- small increments between ability levels
- helpful feedback
- good record-keeping capabilities
- simulations of real-life solutions
- tool capabilities

As with calculators, it is important to instruct students on how to use computers, and when they are appropriately used in the classroom. Computers and software should be accessible to students and in good working order.

CONCLUSION

The strategies discussed throughout this chapter will be of particular benefit to students with learning disabilities. In summary, students will benefit when teachers

- teach and adapt an appropriate curriculum
- teach both explicitly and constructively
- teach for understanding
- utilize a problem-solving approach
- utilize techniques of effective instruction
- explicitly model thinking and problem-solving strategies
- promote connections and communication
- promote a positive attitude
- use multiple representations
- incorporate technology
- use varied instructional groups

These important elements of mathematics instruction will serve to benefit all students in learning mathematics. It cannot be emphasized too strongly that all students need to develop their own understanding of how they best learn. Using the strategies mentioned throughout his book will help students succeed in a mathematics classroom, but it is also important to help them learn how to help themselves beyond any one classroom and beyond the walls of the school. There are no special "checkout lines for special education students." They inhabit the same world we do and need to function successfully there. Students must consistently expand their repertoire of compensatory strategies to help them throughout life to utilize their mathematical knowledge and develop new knowledge.

Teaching mathematics to include the needs of low achievers and students with learning difficulties is a challenging task. However, it is also rewarding and will make anyone who successfully teaches these children a better teacher, one who can justly be proud of supporting the learning and promoting the success of our most challenged children.

Glossary

Americans With Disabilities Act of 1990 (ADA)   Legislation enacted to prohibit discrimination based on disability.

AD/HD (Attention Deficit Hyperactive Disorder)   A condition identified as a medical diagnosis by the American Psychiatric Association's Diagnostic and Statistical Manual III-Revised (DSM III-R). This condition is also often called Attention Deficit Disorder (ADD) because of that usage in a previous edition of DSM. Although it is not a service category under IDEA, children with this condition may be eligible for service under other categories or under Section 504.

Affective   A term that refers to emotions and attitudes.

Assessment   Systematic method of obtaining information from tests or other sources; procedures used to determine child's eligibility for special services, identify the child's strengths and needs, and services child needs to meet these needs.

Auditory discrimination   The ability to detect differences in sounds, such as differences made by the sounds of the letters "m" and "n."

Cognitive   A term that refers to reasoning or intellectual capacity.

Disability   In Section 504 and ADA, defined as impairment that substantially affects one or more major life activities; an individual who has a record of having such impairment, or is regarded as having such an impairment.

Discrimination   The process of detecting differences between and/or among stimuli.

Expressive language   Communication through writing, speaking, and/or gestures.

Fine motor   Functions which require tiny muscle movements, for example, writing or typing.

IDEA (Individuals With Disabilities Education Act)   Law that modifies and extends the Education for All Handicapped Children Act (EHA). Amended in 1997.

Inclusion   A philosophical position based upon the belief that there is one educational system for all students, and that every student is entitled to an instructional program that meets his or her individual needs and learning characteristics. In practice, the term has come to refer to teaching and meeting needs of special-education students within the regular classroom.

Individualized Education Plan (IEP)   A written educational prescription developed for each handicapped (including learning-disabled) student. Generally referred to as an Individualized Education Plan, school districts are required by law to develop these plans in conjunction with the parents.

Learning disabilities   The term "specific learning disability," usually shortened to "learning disability," or LD, refers to a disorder in one or more of the basic psychological processes involved in understanding or in using language (spoken or written), which may manifest itself in an imperfect ability to listen, speak, read, write, spell, or to do mathematical calculations. The term includes such conditions as perceptual handicaps, brain injury, minimal brain dysfunction, dyslexia, and developmental aphasia. Under law, the term does not include children who have learning disabilities that are primarily the result of visual, hearing, or motor handicaps, mental retardation, emotional disturbance, or are the result of environmental, cultural, or economic disadvantage.

Least Restrictive Environment (LRE)   A federal mandate that to the maximum extent appropriate, children with disabilities be educated with children who are not disabled.

Mainstreaming   The process of placing special needs students for at least part of the day into regular education classrooms. This is a term that predates the term inclusion. The term inclusion has come to extend to mainstreaming, too, although technically it means inclusion in regular classrooms for all classes, whereas mainstreaming is a mixture of regular classroom and special education classes.

Modification   Changes in curriculum or instruction that substantially change the requirements of the class or substantially alter the content standards or benchmarks.

Perceptual abilities   The abilities to process, organize, and interpret the information obtained by the five senses; a function of the brain.

Perseveration   The repeating of words, tasks, or motions. A student who has difficulty shifting from one task to a new task.

Public Law 94–142   The 1975 Federal Education for All Handicapped Children Act which requires each state to provide a free and appropriate education to all children from birth through age 21.

Receptive language   Language that is spoken or written by others and received by an individual. These skills include reading and listening.

Regular education   All education except special education.

Reversals   Term used to refer to difficulty in reading or reproducing letters alone, letters in words, or words in sentences in their proper position in space or in proper order. May also refer to reversal of mathematical concepts (add/subtract; multiply/divide) and symbols (>; x+).

Special Education (SPED)   Specially designed instruction, at no cost to the parents, to meet the unique needs of an eligible individual, includes the specially designed instruction conducted in schools, in the home, in hospitals and institutions, and in other settings. Special education offers a continuum of services in order to provide for the education needs of each eligible individual regardless of the nature or severity of those needs.

References

Ackerman, P. T., Anhalt, J. M., & Dykman, R. A. (1986). Arithmetic automatization failure in children with attention and reading disorders: Association and sequelae. *Journal of Learning Disabilities, 19,* 222–232.

Americans with Disabilities Act of 1990, 42 U.S.C. § 12101 et. seq.

American Psychiatric Association. (2000). *Diagnostic and statistical manual of mental disorders* (4th ed., text revision). Washington, DC: Author.

Babbitt, B. C. (1999). *10 Tips for Software Selection for Math Instruction* [Online]. Available: http://www.ldonline.org/ld_indepth/technology/babbitt_math_tips.html

Babbitt, B. C., & Miller, S. P. (1997). Using hypermedia to improve the mathematics problem-solving skills of students with learning disabilities. In K. Higgins & R. Boone (Eds.), *Technology for students with learning disabilities* (pp. 91–108). Austin, TX: Pro-Ed.

Baroody, A. J., & Bartels, B. H. (2000). Using concept maps to link mathematical ideas. *Mathematics Teaching in the Middle School, 5*(9), 604–609.

Baxter, J. A., Woodward, J., & Olson, D. (2001). Effects of reform-based mathematics instruction on low achievers in five third-grade classrooms. *The Elementary School Journal, 101*(5), 529–547.

Baxter, J. A, Woodward, J., Olson, D., & Robyns, J. (2002). Blueprint for Writing in Middle School Mathematics. *Mathematics Teaching in the Middle School 8*(1), 52–56.

Bley, N. S., & Thornton, C. A. (1995) *Teaching mathematics to students with learning disabilities.* Austin, TX: Pro-Ed.

Borkowski, J. G. (1992). Metacognitive theory: A framework for teaching literacy, writing, and math skills. *Journal of Learning Disabilities, 25* (4), 253–257.

Bos, C. S., & Vaughn, S. (1994). *Strategies for teaching students with learning and behavior problems* (3rd ed.). Boston: Allyn & Bacon.

Bottge, B. A. (2001). Reconceptualizing mathematics problem solving for low-achieving students. *Remedial and Special Education, 22* (2), 102–112.

Bottge, B. A., & Hasselbring, T. S. (1993). A comparison of two approaches for teaching complex, authentic mathematics problems to adolescents in remedial mathematics classes. *Exceptional Children, 59*(6), 556–566.

Brian, T., Bay, M., Lopez-Reyna, N., & Donahue, M. (1991). Characteristics of students with learning disabilities: A summary of the extant database and its implications for educational programs. In J. W. Lloyd, N. Nirbhay, & A. C. Repp (Eds.), *The regular education initiative: Alternative perspectives on concepts, issues, and models* (pp.113–131). Sycamore, IL: Sycamore.

131

Brown, A. L., & Campione, J. C. (1990). Communities of learning and thinking, or a context by any other name. In D. Kuhn (Ed.), *Contributions to Human Development, 21*, 108–125.

Brownell, M. T., Mellard, D. F., & Deshler, D. D. (1993). Differences in the learning and transfer performances between students with learning disabilities and other low achieving students on problem-solving tasks. *Learning Disability Quarterly, 16*, 138–156.

Bryant, D. P., Bryant, B. R, & Hammill, D. D. (2000). Characteristic behaviors of students with LD who have teacher-identified math weaknesses. *Journal of Learning Disabilities, 33* (2), 168–177.

Cassel, J., & Reid, R. (1996). Use of a self-regulated strategy intervention to improve word problem-solving skills of students with mild disabilities. *Journal of Behavioral Education, 6*, 153–172.

Cawley, J. F., & Miller, J. H. (1989). Cross-sectional comparisons of the mathematical performance of children with learning disabilities: Are we on the right track toward comprehensive programming? *Journal of Learning Disabilities, 23*, 250–254, 259.

Cawley, J. F., Parmar, R. S., Yan, W., & Miller, J. H. (1998). Arithmetic computations performance of students with learning disabilities: Implications for curriculum. *Learning Disabilities Research & Practice, 13*(2), 68–74.

Clements, D. H. (2000). Translating lessons from research into mathematics classrooms: Mathematics and special needs students. *Perspectives, 26*(3), 31–33.

Clements, D. H., & Battista, M. T. (1989). Learning of geometric concepts in a Logo environment. *Journal for Research in Mathematics Education, 20*(5), 450–467.

Clements, D. H., & McMillen, S. (1996). Rethinking "concrete" manipulatives. *Teaching Children Mathematics, 2*(5), 270–279.

Cobb, P., Yackel, E., & Wood, T. (1992). A constructivist alternative to the representational view of mind in mathematics education. *Journal for Research in Mathematics Education, 23*(1), 2–33.

Connolly, P. (1989). Writing and the ecology of learning. In P. Connolly & T. Valardi (Eds.), *Writing to learn mathematics and science* (pp. 1–14). New York: Teachers College Press.

Education for All Handicapped Children Act of 1975. Public Law 94–142 (1975).

Englert, C. S., Culatta, B. E., & Horn, D. G. (1987). Influence of irrelevant information in addition word problems on problem solving. *Learning Disability Quarterly, l0*, 29–36.

Etheredge, S. (2000). Word problems: A structure-plus-writing approach. *Perspectives, 26*(3), 22–25.

Fasko, S. N. (1994). *The effects of a peer tutoring program on math fact recall and generalization.* Paper presented at the American Psychological Association, Los Angeles.

Fleischner, J. E., Garnett, K., & Shepherd, M. J. (1982). Proficiency in arithmetic basic fact computation of learning disabled and nondisabled children. *Focus on Learning Problems In Mathematics 4*, 47–55.

Fleischner, J. E., Nuzum, M., & Marzola, E. (1987). Devising an instructional program to teach arithmetic problem-solving skills to students with learning disabilities. *Journal of Learning Disabilities, 20*, 214–217.

French, N. K. (1998). Working together: Resource teachers and paraeducators. *Remedial and Special Education, 19*(6), 365.

French, N. K. (2002). Paraeducators: Who are they and what do they do? *Teaching Exceptional Children, 32*(1), 65–69.

Fuchs, L., & Fuchs, D. (1988). Curriculum-based measurement: A methodology for evaluating and improving student programs. *Diagnostique, 14*, 3–13.

Fuchs, L. S., Fuchs, D., Hamlett, C. L., Phillips, N. B., Karnes, K., & Dutka, S. (1997). Enhancing students' helping behavior during peer-mediated instruction with conceptual mathematical explanations. *Elementary School Journal, 97*(3), 223–249.

Fuchs, L. S., Fuchs, D., Karnes, K. (2001). Enhancing kindergartners' mathematical development: Effects of peer-assisted learning strategies. *The Elementary School Journal, 101*(5), 495–510.

Gagne, E. D., Yerkovich, C. W. & Yerkovich, F. R. (1993) *The cognitive psychology of school learning.* New York: HarperCollins.

Gagnon, J. C., & Maccini, P. (2001). Preparing students with disabilities for algebra. *Teaching exceptional children, 34*(1), 8–15.

Garnett, K. (1992). Developing fluency with basic number facts: Intervention for students with learning disabilities. *Learning Disabilities Research & Practice, 7*, 210–216.

Garofalo, J., & Lester, F. K. (1985) Metacognition, cognitive monitoring, and mathematical performance. *Journal for Research in Mathematics Education, 16*(3), 163–76.

Geary, D. C. (1993). Mathematical disabilities: Cognitive, neuropsychological, and genetic components. *Psychological Bulletin, 114*(2), 345–362.

Geary, D. C. (1999). *Mathematical Disabilities: What We Know and Don't Know.* [Online]. Available: http://www.ldonline.org/ld_indepth/math_skills/geary_math_dis.html

Geary, D. C. (2000). Mathematical disorders: An overview for educators. *Perspectives, 26*(3), 6–9.

Geary, D. C., Hamson, C. O., & Hoard, M. K. (2000). Numerical and arithmetic cognition: A longitudinal study of process and concept deficits in children with learning disabilities. *Journal of Experimental Child Psychology, 77*(3), 236–263.

Geary, D. C., Hoard, M. K., & Hamson, C. O. (1999). Numerical and arithmetic cognition: Patterns of functions and deficits in children at risk for a mathematical disability. *Journal of Experimental Child Psychology, 74*(3), 213–239.

Gersten, R., Carnine, D., & Woodward, J. (1987). Direct instruction research: The third decade. *Remedial and Special Education, 8*(6), 48–56.

Gersten, R., & Chard, D. (1999). Number sense: Rethinking arithmetic Instruction for students with mathematical disabilities. *The Journal of Special Education, 33* (1), 18–28.

Greeno, J. G. (1993). For research to reform education and cognitive science. In L. A. Penner, G. M. Batsche, H. M. Knoff, & D. L. Nelson (Eds.), *The challenge in mathematics and science education: Psychology's response* (pp. 153–192). Washington, DC: American Psychological Association.

Greeno, J. G. (1998), & The Middle School Mathematics Through Applications Project Group. The situativity of knowing, learning, and research. *American Psychologist, 53*(1), 5–26.

Griffin, S, & Case, R. (1997). Re-thinking the primary school math curriculum: An approach based on cognitive science. *Issues in Education, 4,* 1–51.

Haager, D., & Vaughn, S. (1995). Parent, teacher, peer, and self-reports of the social competence of students with learning disabilities. *Journal of Learning Disabilities, 28*(4), 205–215.

Haberman, M. (1991). The pedagogy of poverty verses good teaching. *Phi Delta Kappan,* 290–294.

Harper, G. F., Mallette, B., Maheady, L., Bentley, A. E., & Moore, J. (1995). Retention and treatment failure in classwide peer tutoring: Implications for future research. *Journal of Behavioral Education, 5,* 399–414.

Harris, C. A., Miller, S. P., & Mercer, C. D. (1995). Teaching initial multiplication skills to students with disabilities in general education classrooms. *Learning Disabilities Research & Practice, 10,* 180–195.

Heddens, J. W., & Speer, W. (1988). Today's mathematics: Concepts and methods in elementary school mathematics. *Teaching Children Mathematics,* 58.

Hembree, R., & Dessart. D. J. (1992). Research on calculators in mathematics education. In J. T. Fey & C. R. Hirsch (Eds.), *Calculators in mathematics education, 1992 yearbook of the National Council of Teachers of Mathematics (NCTM),* pp. 23–32. Reston, VA.

Herbert, E. (1985). One point of view: Manipulatives are good mathematics. *Arithmetic Teacher, 38*(2), 22–23.

Hiebert, J., & Carpenter, T. (1992). Learning and teaching with understanding. In D. A. Grouws (Ed.), *Handbook of research on mathematics teaching and learning* (pp. 65–97). New York: Macmillan.

Hutchinson, N. L. (1993a). Effects of cognitive strategy instruction on algebra problem solving of adolescents with learning disabilities. *Learning Disability Quarterly, 16*(1), 34–63.

Hutchinson, N. L (1993b). Second invited response: Students with disabilities and mathematics education reform—Let the dialogue begin. *Remedial and Special Education, 14*(6), 20–23.

Individuals With Disabilities Education Act, 20 U.S.C. §1400 et seq. (1997).

Jetter, A. (1993, February 21). Mississippi learning. *The New York Times Magazine,* pp. 288–35, 50, 51, 64, 72.

Johnson, D. W., & Johnson, R. T. (1986). Mainstreaming and cooperative learning strategies. *Exceptional Children, 52*(6), 553–561.

Kluth, P., Villa, R. A, & Thousand, J. S. (2002). Our school doesn't offer inclusion and other legal blunders. *Educational Leadership, 59*(4), 24–27.

Leibson, C. L, Katusic, S. K., Barbaresi, W. J., Ransom, J., O'Brien, J. B. (2001). *Journal of the American Medical Association, 285*(1), pp. 60–66.

Licht, B. (1993). Achievement-related beliefs in children with learning disabilities: Impact on motivation and strategic learning. In L. Melzer (Ed.), *Strategy assessment and instruction for students with learning disabilities: From theory to practice* (pp. 195–220). Austin, TX: Pro-Ed.

Licht, B., & Dweck, C. S. (1984). Determinants of academic achievement: The interaction of children's achievement orientations with skill area. *Developmental Psychology, 20*(4), 628–636.

Lock, R. H. (1996). *Adapting mathematics instruction in the general education classroom for students with mathematics disabilities* [Online]. Available: http://www.ldonline.org/ld_indepth/math_skills/adapt_cld.html

Maccini, P., & Gagnon, J. C. (2000). Best practices for teaching mathematics to secondary students with special needs. *Focus on Exceptional Children, 32*(5), 1–21.

Maccini, P., & Gagnon, J. C. (2002). Perceptions and application of the NCTM standards by special and general education teachers. *Exceptional Children, 68*(3), 325–344.

Maccini, P., & Hughes, C. A. (2000). Effects of a problem solving strategy on the introductory algebra performance of secondary students with learning disabilities. *Learning Disabilities Research and Practice, 15,* 10–21.

Marolda, M. R. (2000). Challenges in learning and teaching mathematics. *Perspectives, 26*(3), 4–5.

Mastropieri, M. A., Scruggs, T. E., & Shiah, S. (1991). Mathematics instruction for learning disabled students: A review of research. *Learning Disabilities Research & Practice, 6*(2), 89–98.

McLeod, D. B. (1988). Affective issues in mathematical problem solving: Some theoretical considerations. *Journal for Research in Mathematics Instruction, 19*(2), 134–141.

McLeod, T., & Armstrong, S. (1982). Learning disabilities in mathematics—skill deficits and remedial approaches at the intermediate and secondary grades. *Learning Disability Quarterly, 5*(3), 305–311.

McLeskey, J., Henry, D., & Hodges, D. (1999). Inclusion : What progress is being made across disability categories? *Teaching Exceptional Children, 33*(5), 56–62.

Mehring, T. A., & Banikowski, A. K. (2002). Strategies to enhance memory in students with disabilities. *Today, 9*(1), 10–11.

Meltzer, L. J. (1993). *Strategy assessment and instruction for students with learning disabilities.* Austin, TX: Pro-Ed.

Mercer, C. D., Jordan, L., & Miller, S. P. (1996). Implications of constructivism for teaching math to students with mild to moderate disabilities. *The Journal of Special Education, 28*(3), 290–306.

Mercer, C. D. (1997). *Students with learning disabilities* (5th ed.). Upper Saddle River, NJ: Prentice Hall/Merrill.

Mercer, C. D., & Mercer, A. R. (1998). *Teaching students with learning problems* (5th ed.). Upper Saddle River, NJ: Prentice Hall/Merrill.

Mercer, C. D., & Miller, S. P. (1992). Teaching students with learning problems in math to acquire, understand, and apply basic math facts. *Remedial and Special Education, 13*(3), 19–35, 61.

Mtetwa, D., & Garofalo, J. (1989). Beliefs about mathematics: An overlooked aspect of student difficulties. *Academic Therapy, 24*(5), 611–618.

Miller, S. P., & Mercer, C. D. (1997). Educational aspects of mathematical disabilities. *Journal of Learning Disabilities, 30*(1), pp. 47–56.

Miller, S. P., Butler, F. M., Lee, K. (1998). Validated practices for teaching mathematics to students with learning disabilities: A review of the literature. *Focus on Exceptional Children, 31*(1), pp. 1–24.

Montague, M., Applegate, B., & Marquard, K. (1993). Cognitive strategy instruction and mathematical problem solving performance of students with learning disabilities. *Learning Disabilities Research and Practice, 8*(4), 223–232.

Montague, M., Bos, C., & Doucette, M. (1991). Affective, cognitive, and metacognitive attributes of eighth grade mathematical problem solvers. *Learning Disabilities Research & Practice, 6*(3), 145–151.

Montague, M. (1993). Student-centered or strategy-centered instruction: What is our purpose? *Journal of Learning Disabilities, 26*(7), 433–437.

Montague, M. (1997). Student perception, mathematical problem solving, and learning disabilities. *Remedial and Special Education, 18*(1), 46–53.

National Center for Educational Statistics. (1996). *Pursuing excellence, NCES 97-198* (initial findings from the Third International Mathematics and Science Study). Available: www.ed.gov/NCES?timss. Washington, DC: U.S. Government Printing Office.

National Research Council (2001). *Adding it up: Helping children learn mathematics.* Washington, DC: National Academy Press.

National Council on Disability. (2000, January 25). *Back to school on civil rights.* (NCD # 00-283). Washington, DC: Author.

National Council of Teachers of Mathematics (1989). *Curriculum and evaluation standards for school mathematics.* Reston, VA: Author.

National Council of Teachers of Mathematics (1991). *Professional standards for teaching mathematics.* Reston, VA: Author.

National Council of Teachers of Mathematics. (2000). *Principles and standards for school mathematics.* Reston, VA: Author.

National Council of Teachers of Mathematics. (1999). *Mathematics assessment: A practical handbook for grades 6–8.* Reston, VA: Author.

Olsen, J. L., & Platt, J. M. (1996). *Teaching children and adolescents with special needs* (3rd ed.). Upper Saddle River, NJ: Prentice Hall.

Patten, J. R., Cronin, M. E., Bassett, D. S., & Koppel, A. E. (1997). A life skills approach to mathematics instruction. Preparing students with learning disabilities. *Journal of Learning Disabilities, 30,* 178–187.

Parmar, R. S., & Cawley, J. F. (1991). Challenging the routines and passivity that characterize arithmetic instruction for children with mild handicaps. *Remedial and Special Education, 12*(5), 23–32, 43.

Parmar, R. S., Cawley, J. F., & Frazita, R. R. (1996). Word problem-solving by students with and without mild disabilities. *Exceptional Children, 62*(5), 415–429.

Polloway, E. A., & Patten, J. R. (2001). Strategies for teaching learners with special needs (7th ed.). NY: Merrill.

Polya, G. (1962). *Mathematical discovery: On understanding, learning, and teaching problem solving* (Vol. 2). New York: Wiley.

Pugalee, D. K. (1997). Connecting writing to the mathematics curriculum. *Mathematics Teacher, 90*(4), 308–310.

Pugalee, D. K., DiBiase, W. J., & Wood, K. D. (1999). Writing and the development of problem solving in mathematics and science. *Middle School Journal 30*(5), 48–52.

Rachlin, S. (1998). Learning to see the wind. *Mathematics Teaching in the Middle School, 3*(7), 470–473.

Rehabilitation Act of 1973, 29 U.S.C. § 701 et. seq.

Rivera, D. P., Gillam, R., Goodwin, M., & Smith, R. (1996). *The effects of cooperative learning on the acquisition of story problem solving skills of students with learning disabilities* (in press).

Rivera, D. P., Taylor, R. L., & Bryant, B. R. (1994/1995). Review of current trends in mathematics assessment for students with mild disabilities. *Diagnostique, 20*(1-4), 143–174.

Rivera, D. P. (1996, Spring). Using cooperative learning to teach mathematics to students with learning disabilities. *LD Forum, 21*(3), 29–33.

Rivera, D. M., & Smith, D. D. (1988). Using a demonstration strategy to teach middle school students with learning disabilities how to compute long division. *Journal of Learning Disabilities, 21,* 77–81.

Robinson, C. S., Menchetti, B. M, & Torgesen, J. K. (2002). Toward a two factor theory of one type of mathematics disabilities. *Learning Disabilities Research & Practice, 17*(2), 81–89.

Rudnitsky, A., Etheredge, S., Freeman, S. J. M., & Gilbert, T. (1995). Learning to solve addition and subtraction word problems through a structure-plus-writing approach. *Journal for Research in Mathematics Education, 26*(5), 467–486.

Schulz, J. B., & Carpenter, C. D. (1995). *Mainstreaming exceptional students.* Needham Heights, MA: Allyn & Bacon.

Schumm, J., Vaughn, S., Haager, D., McDowell, J., Rothlein, L., & Saumell, L. (1995). General education teacher planning: What can students with learning disabilities expect? *Exceptional Children, 61*(4), 335–352.

Scruggs, T., & Mastropieri, M. (1996). Teacher perceptions of mainstreaming/inclusion, 1958–1995: A research synthesis. *Exceptional Children, 63*(1), 59–64.

Shriner, J. G., Kim, D., Thurlow, M. L., & Ysseldyke, J. E. (1993). *IEP's and standards: What they say for students with disabilities* (Tech. Rep. No. 5). Minneapolis, MN: National Center on Educational Outcomes. (ERIC Document Reproduction Service No. ED 358659)

Schoenfeld, A. H. (1985). Metacognitive and epistemological issues in mathematical understanding. In E. A. Silver (Ed.), *Teaching and learning mathematics problem solving: Multiple research perspectives* (pp. 361–379). Mahwah, NJ: Erlbaum.

Schifter, D. (1999). Reasoning about operations: Early algebraic thinking in grades K–6. In L. V. Stiff (Ed.), *Developing mathematical reasoning in grades K–12* (pp. 62–81). Reston, VA: National Council of Teachers of Mathematics.

Sierpinska, A. (1998). Three epistemologies, three views of classroom communication: Constructivism, sociocultural approaches, interactionism. In H. Steinbring, M. Bussi, & A. Sierpinska (Eds.), *Language and communication in the mathematics classroom.* (pp. 30–62). Reston, VA: National Council of Teachers of Mathematics.

Slavin, R. E., Madden, N. A., & Leavy, M. (1984). Effects of team assisted individualization on the mathematics achievement of academically handicapped and non-handicapped students. *Journal of Educational Psychology, 76*(5), 813–819.

Sliva, J. A., & Roddick, C. (2001). Mathematics autobiographies: A window into beliefs, values, and past mathematics experiences of preservice teachers. *Academic Exchange Quarterly, 5*(2), 101–107.

Smith, C. R. (1994). *Learning disabilities: The interaction of learner, task, and setting* (3rd ed.). Boston: Allyn & Bacon.

Smith, T. E. (2001). What educators need to know. *Remedial and Special Education, 22*(6), 335–343.

Smith, D. D., & Luckasson, R. (1992). *Introduction to special education: Teaching in an age of challenge.* Boston: Allyn & Bacon.

Speer, W. R., & Brahier, D. J. (1994). Rethinking the teaching and learning of mathematics. In C. A. Thornton & N. S. Bley (Eds.), *Windows of opportunity: Mathematics for students with special needs* (pp. 41–59). Reston, VA: National Council of Teachers of Mathematics.

Stein, M., Silbert, J., & Carnine, D. (1997). *Designing effective mathematics instruction: A direct instruction approach* (3rd. ed.). Upper Saddle River, NJ: Merrill/Prentice Hall.

Stigler, J. W., & Hiebert, J. (1999). *The teaching gap: Best ideas from the world's teachers for improving education in the classroom.* New York: The Free Press.

Swanson, H. L. (1987). Information processing theory and learning disabilities: An overview. *Journal of Learning Disabilities, 20,* 3–7.

Taylor, R. L. (1993). *Assessment of exceptional students* (3rd ed.). Needham Heights, MA: Allyn & Bacon.

Thornton, C. A., & Jones, G. A. (1996). Adapting instruction for students with special learning needs, K–8. *Journal of Education, 178*(2), 59–69.

Thurlow, M. L. (2000). Standards-based reform and students with disabilities: Reflections on a decade of change. *Focus on Exceptional Children, 33*(3), 1–15.

U.S. Department of Education (1977). Federal Register, 42:250, p. 65083. (Washington, DC: U.S. Government Printing Office.)

U.S. Department of Education (2000). *Guide to the individualized education program.* Washington, DC: Author. (ERIC Document Reproduction Services, 800-443-3742)

Vispoel, W. P., and Austin, J. R. (1995). Success and failure in junior high school: A critical incident approach to understanding students' attributional beliefs. *American Educational Research Journal, 32*(2): 377–412.

Vygotsky, L. S. (1978). *Mind in society.* Cambridge, MA: Harvard University Press.

Warner, M. M., Alley, G. R., Schumaker, J. B., Deshler, D. D., & Clark, F. L. (1980). *An epidemiological study of learning disabled adolescents in secondary schools: Achievement and ability, socioeconomic status and school experiences.* (Report No. 13). Lawrence: University of Kansas Institute for Research in Learning Disabilities.

Wheatley, G. H., & Clements, D. H. (1990). Calculators and constructivism. *Arithmetic Teacher, 38*(2), 22–23.

Wilson, C. L., & Sindelar, P. T. (1991). Direct instruction in math word problems: Students with learning disabilities. *Exceptional Children, 57*(6), 512–519.

Witzel, B., Smith, S. W., & Brownell, M. T. (2001). How can I help students with learning disabilities in Algebra? *Intervention in School and Clinic, 37*(2), 101–104.

Wood, J. (1998). *Adapting instruction to accommodate students in inclusive settings* (3rd. ed.). Upper Saddle River, NJ: Merrill/Prentice Hall.

Woodward, J., Baxter, J., & Robinson, R. (1999). Rules and reasons: Decimal instruction for academically low achieving students. *Learning Disabilities Research & Practice, 14*(1), 15–24.

Xin, P. X., & Jitendra, A. K. (1999). The effects of instruction in solving mathematical word problems for students with learning problems: A meta-analysis. *The Journal of Special Education, 32*(4), 207–225.

Yasutake, D., & Bryant, T. (1995). The influence of affect on the achievement and behavior of students with learning disabilities. *Journal of Learning Disabilities, 28*(6), 329–334.

Zentall, S. S., & Ferkis, M. A. (1993). Mathematical problem solving for youth with ADD, with and without learning disabilities. *Learning Disability Quarterly, 16*, 6–18.

Zorfass, J., & Copel, H. (1995). The I-search: Guiding students toward relevant research. *Educational Leadership, 53*(1), 48–51.

Index

**CORWIN
PRESS**

The Corwin Press logo—a raven striding across an open book—represents the union of courage and learning. Corwin Press is committed to improving education for all learners by publishing books and other professional development resources for those serving the field of K-12 education. By providing practical, hands-on materials, Corwin Press continues to carry out the promise of its motto: **"Helping Educators Do Their Work Better."**